The Retr

Also in the same series:

Seeing Ourselves – interpreting contemporary society

Libby Purves, Robert Blake, Danah
Zohar & John Habgood

The Retreat of the State

Nigel Lawson, Arthur Seldon, Michael Taylor & David Owen

edited with a preface and afterword by
Stephen Platten
and with an introduction by
Vincent Watts

CANTERBURY
PRESS
Norwich

© Nigel Lawson, Arthur Seldon, Michael Taylor, David Owen,
Vincent Watts and Stephen Platten 1998

First published in 1999 by The Canterbury Press Norwich
(a publishing imprint of Hymns Ancient & Modern Limited,
a registered charity)
St Mary's Works, St Mary's Plain
Norwich, Norfolk, NR3 3BH

British Library Cataloguing in Publication Data

A catalogue record for this book is available
from the British Library

ISBN 1-85311-258-5

Typeset by Rowland Phototypesetting,
Bury St Edmunds, Suffolk
Printed in Great Britain by
Biddles Ltd, Guildford and King's Lynn

Contents

Contributors

Lord Lawson is an economist and was successively a financial journalist, Fellow of Nuffield College, Oxford, and Chancellor of the Exchequer from 1983 to 1989.

Dr Arthur Seldon is an economist and writer and is a Founder President of the Institute of Economic Affairs.

The Revd Michael Taylor was Principal of the Northern Baptist College, and Director of Christian Aid and is now President of the Selly Oak Colleges in Birmingham.

Lord Owen was Foreign and Commonwealth Secretary from 1977 to 1979, Leader of the Social Democratic Party from 1983 to 1987 and Co-Chairman of the International Conference on the former Yugoslavia from 1992 to 1998.

Preface

The essays gathered together in this book began in a
slightly different form as the second series of Launcelot
Fleming Lectures sponsored by Norwich Cathedral and
the University of East Anglia in the autumn of 1998.
Launcelot Fleming was Bishop of Norwich during the
1960s and formed a strong and fruitful relationship
between the church and the burgeoning university at
that time. His broad sympathies, his Christian human-
ism and his commitment to wide cultural interests are
the reasons why this annual set of lectures was dedicated
to his name. Each year we attempt to explore a topic
that engages with society as widely as possible and is
also one to which we bring at least some theological
critique.

In the past few years there has been an increasing
assumption that government has become too *big* and
that the state should pull back from too great an involvement in a variety of different aspects of life, both
nationally and internationally. The 1998 Fleming Lectures addressed this perception and asked whether it is
a true assessment of trends over the past twenty years.
To the four main essays there has been added an Introduction by Vincent Watts, the present Vice-Chancellor

of the University of East Anglia, and I have written a brief Afterword. We hope that this book will be a contribution to a continuing debate.

Stephen Platten
Norwich
June 1999

Abbreviations

DFID	Department for International Development
EMS	European Monetary System
EMU	Economic and Monetary Union/ European Monetary Union
ERM	Exchange-Rate Mechanism
EU	European Union
GATT	General Agreement on Tariffs and Trade
GDP	Gross Domestic Product
GNP	Gr oss National Product
IMF	International Monetary Fund
LETS	Local Exchange and Trading Systems
MAI	Multilateral Agreement on Investment
NATO	North Atlantic Treaty Organization
NGOs	Non-Governmental Organizations
NHS	National Health Service
OECD	Organization for Economic Co-operation and Development
SPD	Sozialdemokratische Partei Deutschlands (the German Social Democratic Party)
UK	United Kingdom
UN	United Nations
USA	United States of America
WEU	Western European Union
World Bank	International Bank for Reconstruction and Development

Introduction

VINCENT WATTS

In May 1997, at the end of a long period of Conservative government, our nation state, the United Kingdom (UK), was stable but seen by many as under threat from the growing power of the European Union (EU) to interfere in our domestic affairs. By May 1999, after two years of Labour government, radical change had been started – an elected parliament in Scotland, and an elected assembly in Wales and in Northern Ireland. A referendum had been held which committed London to an elected mayor. England had been set on the path to a stronger regional structure with the launch of the Regional Development Agencies and a central government commitment to introduce, after consulting the people of each English region, elected regional assemblies. This example, which could be repeated for many other countries, illustrates the speed of change in the role of nation states and their governments.

More globally, the European Union is going through change as the European Parliament seeks to enforce its power over the European Commission. The North Atlantic Treaty Organization (NATO) for the first time in its history attacked a European country because we could not let this sort of behaviour (the ethnic cleansing of Kosovo by the Serbian army) happen in Europe. The following chapters examine the notion that the role of nation states, which has increased rapidly in developed countries during the twentieth century, has now reached a peak, and is beginning to retreat. The powers accumulated by nation states are being shared with, or handed over to, the private sector, regional bodies, or multinational organizations or being removed by actions of large multinational corporations or global markets. What, then, do the contributors have to say about this scenario?

The Contributors

Lord Lawson

Lord Lawson brought to the Conservative government led by Margaret Thatcher in 1979 the trained mind of a Philosophy, Politics and Economics graduate from Oxford University, the experience of interacting with economic events from the financial editorial chair of a major national newspaper, and a commitment to liberal economics. He shaped many of the economic policies of that government in which he served in a number of ministerial roles, culminating as Chancellor of the Exchequer. He continued his involvement in economic affairs as a director of a major UK bank. His chapter, 'The Retreat of the State in Economic Management', is a masterly distillation of this experience and a powerful advocacy on pragmatic grounds for economic liberalism.

Introduction

Arthur Seldon

In his chapter, 'The Retreat of the State in Social Welfare', Arthur Seldon brings his wide experience to bear on the history and issues relating to social welfare, how governments have arrived at the present position, why this position is no longer tenable, and some possible ways forward.

Michael Taylor

Michael Taylor's chapter, 'The Retreat of the State from Overseas Development', reflects the turnaround in UK policy on this important issue. At the time when this book was being planned, most governments were cutting their commitments to overseas development, but by the time Michael Taylor wrote his chapter we had a renewed commitment in the UK in the form of the White Paper *Eliminating World Poverty: A challenge for the 21st Century*.[1] Many of the themes he develops are similar to those mentioned by Lord Lawson and Arthur Seldon. He adds to these themes a distinction between the nature of the countries of the North (the developed world), and countries of the South. In the North, as we will discuss, the state is changing its role but not retreating overall. The Northern states are well able to take on the multinationals, collect taxes which are a growing share of their Gross Domestic Products (GDPs), and manage (more or less competently) programmes of social change. The relatively weak Southern states are buffeted by the multinationals, the currency and the bond

3

markets, and are unable to control with integrity their citizens. This severely limits the ability of the North to help the South. Michael Taylor also expresses concerns about the way Northern governments are reducing their involvement with Non-Governmental Organizations (NGOs). In part, governments are doing this because of their concern that charitable giving is postponing the development of the Southern states' own ability to manage their affairs. He concludes with a Christian view based on his experience as the Director of Christian Aid.

Lord Owen

Lord Owen started his career as a doctor at St Thomas's Hospital. He then entered politics and rose to become Foreign Secretary. Subsequently he had a major role in seeking to bring about a peaceful resolution of one of the most intractable problems in Europe, the dismemberment of Yugoslavia. His chapter, 'The Retreat of the State in International Affairs', covers the issue of national sovereignty, especially that of the UK and the United States of America (USA). He examines the role played by both countries in international affairs and the extent to which they do and should surrender some of their sovereignty to multinational organizations.

Background

Centuries of experiment and debate have developed two main concepts of the state. First there is the civil association model, in which the role of the state is to enable

4

people to pursue their own lives, to their own objectives without the imposition of some higher aim formulated by the state. In the second model the state is seen as an enterprise, in which the state has aims of its own, such as conquest, religious zeal, social equality, prosperity and so on. This is exemplified in Britain by the use of the term 'UK plc'. Both of these concepts have elements of similarity. In both we would expect to find the rule of law, social controls to dissuade individuals from actions which create damaging externalities, the capacity to defend frontiers and the need to be able to conduct foreign policy. They differ in attitude towards great national programmes, intervention in markets to deal with market failure, and intervention with individuals in response to failure to provide for self and family.

Today we are clearly living our lives within the 'State as Enterprise' concept whether we like it or not. We know how the twentieth century has led us to this destination. Contemporary history tells the tale of a devastating war followed by a severe depression, leading to an even more devastating war, the post-war rebuilding, and the popularity of the welfare state. Financially this has meant a growth of government expenditure in developed countries from a few per cent of GDP to an average for the Organization for Economic Co-operation and Development (OECD) of around 47 percent.

The idea of the 'retreat of the state' has developed over the last two decades. Margaret Thatcher fought hard to reduce the role of the public sector in the UK, and there were similar, but less vigorous efforts by Ronald Reagan in the USA. The collapse of the Soviet

Union in 1989 was seen to demonstrate the failure of extreme government dominance of an economy; the subsequent revelations about how many government enterprises in that country were value subtracting added strength to this message. Globalization of financial markets, where the daily transaction volumes are multiples of the foreign exchange reserves of large countries, has created a belief that the economic destiny of nation states is much less under their control than hitherto. Technology has reduced the cost of transport so that multinational companies have been able to create mobility of skilled personnel and capital assets outside the control of nation states. Information technology has eliminated the ability of nations to censor the communications of their citizens. Television has enabled these citizens to become knowledgeable about the prosperity of others, and to see that other countries have found different, and often better, ways of providing public services. It is also believed that taxation has reached, or in some cases exceeded, the willingness of citizens to pay. Citizens are experimenting with technology, and new ways of doing business, such as barter, to reduce their exposure to the tax collectors.

These relationships between the state, its citizens, and the business enterprises which operate within and between states depend for their operation on orderly relationships between states. A primary function of a nation state is to protect the integrity of its borders, to maintain its sovereignty within these borders and to regulate its relations with other nation states. Two of the chapters are concerned with these issues. The chapter on overseas development touches on these issues within the developing world, the South. Part of the argument here is that states in the South are too weak to handle the forces which buffet them. They are victims of multi-nationals, global capital markets, and the shifting patterns of global trade and investment; equally they are not strong enough to stand up to the corrupting influences of their own citizens. Perhaps for these countries the state needs to be strengthened to handle these demands. The fourth chapter is concerned with another aspect of retreat: the retreat from independent handling of foreign policy by a nation state and the movement towards its sharing of its sovereignty with multinational organizations. A mixture of gains and losses includes a strong plea for the UK never to give up its right for independent action on the international stage.

The purpose of this book is to examine these thoughts. What is the evidence? If the state is in retreat, why is this happening? Where are these trends likely to lead? The contributors are all leaders in terms of influence and with a history of being active in their own fields. Let us first set a context.

Freedom, Democracy and Capitalism

One of the conclusions of a century of economic experiment is the superior ability of the free-market system of capitalism to generate wealth. Nigel Lawson develops and justifies this theme. Economic success is generally greater in countries where the state had interfered least with the free-market system. The free-market system has many disadvantages but experience has shown that interfering with markets to seek to reduce these disadvantages usually generates other problems, and reduces prosperity. One of the most significant of these disadvantages is that the benefits of prosperity are unevenly divided. Economic success is often associated with growing income differentials and does very little for the poor. The income divide risks creating alienated groups who then act via the ballot box and through direct destructive behaviour. The democratic response is progressive taxation and transfer payments to the alienated, and regulation of the economy. This reduces incentives, reduces individual freedom and gums up the works of the 'prosperity-creating' part of society. Experience also indicates that these state interventions rarely achieve the aims of social inclusion, although the interventions may reduce the most antisocial behaviour patterns. Many of the problems remain but the future growth in prosperity which enables other ways to deal with the problems has been undermined.

Once in this position it is difficult to retreat. Arthur Seldon develops this theme. Indeed he puts forward the interesting thought that the growth of government activities has undermined and driven out the individual and collective arrangements which were developing well at the end of the nineteenth century. Perhaps the successive attempts of governments to improve education and to reduce sickness and poverty have destroyed the opportunity for alternative, possibly more successful, approaches. In the Soviet Union it is now well established that the state industries generally subtracted value from their resource inputs and eliminated the possibility of developing a successful private sector and an enterprise culture. Perhaps the welfare state has been similarly value subtracting and may need a similarly radical overhaul. We may be going along a path which will lead us to a dead end (or worse) and which will require us to retrace our steps and start from a very different position.

Much of the growth in public expenditure has been in 'transfer payments and subsidies', particularly in income support, support for the disabled and for single parents and the unemployed; pensions are also part of this wider pattern. In the UK these make up about 25 percent of public expenditure and as yet no viable approach to reducing these costs has emerged. With the growing proportion of people over pension age, the issue facing the state is how to contain the expenditure within current limits. One response of government is to seek to grow the economy while restraining the growth of transfers. This increases the emphasis on the 'State as Enterprise' model and further reduces the freedom of the citizen to follow his own whim. In summary, and oversimplifying, freedom enables capitalism, which generates prosperity and social division. Democracy seeks to reduce social division but in doing so reduces freedom and undermines the prosperity on which government was relying to pay for social inclusion. Finding the right balance between these desirable aims, which have undesirable side effects, is the unsolved problem of today and the challenge of the next decade.

Vincent Watts

Is the Retreat of the State Desirable?

In seeking the best balance between freedom, democracy and capitalism it would be helpful to have some agreement about the desirable direction for change. There are two main schools of thought. Reducing the role of the state will bring benefits. There will be more rapid technological development bringing greater prosperity. Improved prosperity will create a greater opportunity to relieve global poverty. There will be greater personal freedom. The second view argues that the role of the state should not be reduced but that there is scope for redefinition. This school of thought agrees with an increased role of markets and the private sector in service delivery. Technology and, to some extent, ideology are driving change today but these are temporary factors, and the gains are modest. The drawbacks are serious in terms of a less fair society: the losers will be the unskilled who are in any case the least able to look after themselves; poverty could increase amongst those with little to offer, and increased social exclusion may result. These opposed and strongly held views do not give us a clear sense of direction for desirable change. Both sets of views are based on the assumption that the state is retreating. It is not clear that this is really happening.

Is the State Retreating?

In the USA under Reagan and Bill Clinton (the age of 'big government' is dead), the share of GDP taken by government has steadily increased to about 33 percent.

Introduction

Under the uninterrupted period of eighteen years of Conservative government in the UK, led first by Margaret Thatcher and then by John Major, the share of GDP taken by government declined from 43 percent to 42 percent. This achievement involved privatization on a massive scale, successive cuts, and many confrontations with public sector trade unions. Other developed countries which have not pursued such policies have seen their government share of GDP grow to 50 per cent to 55 percent of GDP (Austria, Belgium, Italy, France). There are enormous pressures behind the three big public spending programmes:

- transfer payments and subsidies are difficult to reverse and are strengthened by an ageing population;
- healthcare costs increase as a result of rising expectations, rapid technological developments and again an ageing population;
- education costs increase to enable our people to compete in a more complex world and cope with rapid change.

In the light of these pressures and the electoral popularity of these programmes, the Thatcher achievement of a modest reduction in share of GDP was a very real one. Even in countries where the share of GDP had been held roughly constant, the GDP itself has been growing at a few per cent per annum so the resources available to the state have increased.

Vincent Watts

The state, however, has many other ways of influencing its citizens. These could be summarized as laws and regulations, which have been growing in number much faster than public expenditure and regulate closely the daily lives of citizens, as well as constraining businesses. It is interesting to cite some recent examples of interference in matters which it was previously assumed that adults could decide for themselves: curfews for children, maximum weekly hours of work, and minimum wages. Again there have been attempts to push back the frontiers of the state, but still this has at best been a holding operation.

The reason why the idea of the retreat of the state has gained currency could be that the rate of growth in government expenditure has slowed, and that there have been some notable victories in reducing the role of the state in important areas. The main victories have been in the economic arena and Nigel Lawson describes these successes. The primary area of retreat is from the delivery of services where the view is gaining acceptance that the private sector will generally be more efficient and effective than a government in running operations such as electricity generation, the taxation information technology systems, or constructing hospitals. This shows itself in the form of privatization and 'contractorization' (the delivery of public services through contracts with the private sector).

In summary, the government share of GDP is growing and the pressures are for this to continue. The degree of regulation is increasing and individuals are less able to control their own affairs without interference. Although

12

there is a distinct retreat from the direct delivery of services and in some cases from interference with markets, the overall conclusion has to be that the role of the state is continuing to increase.

The Growing Importance of Regions

The role of the state may be increasing but the way in which this role is being discharged is likely to become more accountable and closer to the people it should be seeking to serve. Europe is becoming more and more based on *regions*. This is one way in which the state is seeking to become more relevant to the people and less remote. This is being driven by several factors: scale, industry structure, and the delivery of more efficient and effective government. It is worth exploring these in a little more detail.

Scale

One of the factors causing the growth of the size of the nation state was the nature of warfare. The significant players on the international stage during the twentieth century have had populations of around forty to fifty million. These had sufficient taxable and manpower capacity to create and equip the armies and navies, which proved successful. Much smaller countries did not have the scale to compete. The cost of this scale was a central government remote from the people. Most democracies had some form of local government, which dealt with local issues. More and more of the decisions became centralized, remote and often not relevant to the needs of the people. However, the prospect of military success, or the threat of failure more than compensated for this remoteness. Remember the way history was taught at school! The role of foreign policy and military strength is now bound up with multinational organizations and alliances and the costs of remoteness are no longer seen as worth the benefit.

Regionalization is rife in Europe. There are many causes. In some cases it is built into the structure, as in federal Germany. In part it helps to give identity to different cultures as in Spain, Belgium and in the United Kingdom. In others, such as France and possibly England, it is more the case of central government delivered through a regional structure. Typically a population unit of around five million people is chosen for a region although cultural or linguistic heritage may create smaller regions.

Industry Structure

The balance between freedom, democracy and capitalism has to be reconsidered in the light of changes in industry structure and the economic success of the USA. The growth in developed economies has largely been in services and this has caused a relative decline in agricultural, extractive and manufacturing industries. In these older industries, economies of scale were plausible and could be seen to more than offset the lack of innovation resulting from the hierarchical structures which fitted easily into large nation states.

Introduction

The new and very profitable industries of information and communications technology, of advanced engineering and of biotechnology thrive on innovation. This is true also of the rapidly growing and nimble 'outsourcers' who provide many of the services on which both new and older industries now rely. There are also the 'creative' industries of film and other media, of advertising and professional services. Innovation and creativity appear to thrive in:

- small rapidly changing organizations, or organizations which can replicate these conditions while growing large;
- a world of start-ups, spin-offs and venture capital;
- a global exchange of ideas and rapid movement of people and capital to the place where it is exciting to be and to work.

Remote and complex governmental organizations are not able to be in sympathy with these needs. As governments seek to increase prosperity and the taxable capacity required to finance the demands for increased expenditure, they have to seek to create structures, which bring together the fast-moving entrepreneurs with the public services, which can support their success. This is being done through public/private sector partnerships where the resources available to the partners are brought together to create environments in which entrepreneurship can thrive, the skills are made available, and compensating programmes are provided to reduce social division. For government to be able to respond to its role in these public/private partnerships it is required to be more efficient and effective in its regional response.

Effective and Efficient Government

Large centralized states inevitably had large centralized bureaucracies. These are alive and well. They continue to attract some of the most able of the nation's young people who pursue their careers based on bureaucratic success. Inevitably the programmes formulated at the national level based on single issue (or small number of issues) policies are unlikely to integrate well to meet the needs of an individual region. This will be exacerbated if the industry structures of the regions are changing at different speeds because of the regional inheritance.

The well-established method of developing policy through wide national consultation and the development of national programmes to implement this policy is too slow and lacks sufficient integration to deliver the government services to support a prosperous modern economy. We will be seeing in many countries the growing strength of regional government and the decentralization of decision making as government seeks to provide new programmes fashioned to respond to the rapid timescales required to create growing prosperity. The public/private partnerships will help accelerate this process. The debate will focus on accountability and on which programmes should be regional and which national rather than on the retreat of the state.

Introduction

Who Will Manage the Regions?

In discussing regions, it tends to be assumed that a national government will continue to have the same autonomy over its territory as it does today. Recent developments question this assumption. The NATO intervention in Kosovo directly challenges the previous long-held belief that nations could do as they wished within their own territorial borders. However, although this is an extreme example, it is not entirely new. The United Kingdom has accepted a role for the USA in helping to bring the situation in Ireland to a peaceful resolution. In both cases there are special reasons, but it could be that we are beginning to see the development of a set of international standards for the behaviour of states or regions and that significant deviation from these standards will be penalized by the international community. In the case of the European Union, the regions are beginning to develop independent access to EU funding and, at present in a small way, to develop ways of diverging from national policies. With the regional election of Members of the European Parliament this could be the beginning of an important development.

Will Competition between States Cause a Retreat?

Although the state has not yet retreated in total, the pressure is on. Skilled labour is mobile and much investment is by multinationals, which are beholden to no state. The growing use of information technology means that people can live where they choose. The architect lives in the Bahamas, agrees his designs remotely and occasionally meets his clients in New York. Already about twenty million people in Europe live in one country and gain their incomes elsewhere. The power of the multinational has been much seen in Europe with the reduction in border controls enabling companies to replace operations in every country with a rationalized structure in about four countries. Often, this is carried out by an internal bidding process, within the company, in which quality and cost are the only criteria. An operation in a country with high taxes/social security costs and unproductive public services will lose the bid. In effect this is putting governments in competition. Those who provide excellent public services at modest cost will win. More investment will occur, jobs will be created and tax revenues will rise. We see this competition in a fierce form when an inward investor is searching for a good deal. This may not cause a retreat of the state but it will put pressure on delivering value for money and it will question the value of redistributive taxation.

In any industry, when competition gets fierce, competitors seek to form cartels. Governments who are interested in free markets try to block such activities. In the case of governments themselves we can already see the cartels forming. In Europe, it is called 'harmonization'. There does not appear to be any institution which has the role of stopping governments conspiring together to create cartels to block competition. If this is the way Euroland is to develop, then will the state be advancing again?

Introduction

Notes

1. Department for International Development, *Eliminating World Poverty: a Challenge for the 21st Century*, White Paper on International Development presented to Parliament by the Secretary of State for International Development ... November 1997, Cm 3789, London, The Stationery Office, 1997.

The Retreat of the State in Economic Management

NIGEL LAWSON

Over the last twenty years of the twentieth century there has been an increasing sense in western society of the shrinkage of government and the movement away from state intervention in a number of areas. It is this assumption that underpins the logic for this book; the other contributors discuss how far this is so in other areas, but I have no doubt that it is true in the economic sphere. It is not so much a case of the retreat of the state *in* economic management, as the retreat of the state *from* economic management, although not, of course, from economic policy altogether; and it is a welcome and long-overdue phenomenon.

Let me make it quite clear that I am not one of those who, whether from the left or the right of the political spectrum, wish to see the withering away of the state. On the contrary, I believe that there remains, and will always remain, a vitally important role for the state – which for all practical purposes will continue to mean the nation state. But it is for this very reason that its retreat in the economic sphere, although neither as extensive nor as irreversible as I would like to see, is in principle welcome. Giving the state powers and res- ponsibilities over and above those which it needs to have is dangerous in two respects: first, it threatens to make the state *too* powerful at the expense of the citizen, and second, by trying to do too much, the state is likely to perform less well those tasks it should be performing. The idea that it is the job of the state to improve the nation's economic performance, nowadays widely seen as its most important role, is in historical terms a very recent notion. A brief, if inevitably oversimplified, excursion into history may be helpful at this point.

Historical Background

From at least Roman times, and for many centuries thereafter, governments intervened in the economy, levying taxation (including duties on imported goods), issuing coinage and preventing others from doing the same, engaging in public works of various kinds, and so on. But all this was done for essentially non-economic reasons – to provide the sinews of war, the framework of the state, and the convenience of rulers or powerful interest groups. Over the centuries too – again for totally non-economic reasons, and to different degrees in differ- ent countries – the power of the state and the privileges of rulers became progressively more circumscribed as the freedoms and liberties of the individual were asserted and secured. By the middle of the eighteenth century it became noticed for the first time that those countries in which the citizen enjoyed the greatest freedom were also those whose people enjoyed the highest standard of living. Thus was born the idea of economic liberalism, whose seminal text was of course Adam Smith's masterpiece, *An Inquiry into the Nature and Causes of the Wealth of Nations*,[1] published in 1776 – the very same year, incidentally, as the American Declaration of Independence and the birth of a nation founded on this new thinking, from which it has benefited hugely ever since. Smith's great achievement was to demonstrate how it was that millions of individuals, without any state direction, freely pursuing their own self-interest within a framework of law (and we will come back to that), could create the public good of a complex and successful national economy.

Now, it was this brilliant insight that, a century later, inspired Darwin's ground-breaking theory, published in *The Origin of Species*,[2] that the complex and wonderful natural order we see all around us can be explained, not in terms of the master plan of a divine directing intelligence, but as the result of myriads of individuals seeking their own survival and, over untold periods of times, adapting to their environment – that is, evolving – in order to do so. Today Darwinism (buttressed by Mendel's theory of genes) enjoys more widespread support than the parallel and earlier insight of Adam Smith. Initially, however, the mid-eighteenth-century idea of economic liberalism – the idea that people should as far as possible be free to spend their money as they wished and to work how and where they wished, and that business should be equally free to produce what they wished and invest what they wished – soon became the prevailing orthodoxy among economists and those in the political classes concerned about economic performance. This idea continued to prevail both in theory and to a considerable extent in practice throughout the nineteenth century, when one particularly important aspect of economic liberalism, *free trade*, became part of the established orthodoxy, accepted by political leaders of all parties, notably in the United Kingdom and the United States, but to a considerable extent in continental Europe, too. The result was a century of outstanding economic, technological, political and civic development.

The Twentieth Century

But the story during the first half of the twentieth century was very different. The First World War, the first total war the world had known, came as a grave shock to the system and caused governments to assume economic powers considered necessary to wage total war. After the war, the apparent malfunctioning of the capitalist free-market economy in the 1920s, and even more the 1930s, marked in particular by unprecedented levels of unemployment, convinced increasing numbers of people that economic liberalism no longer worked, and that the future lay with collectivism and large-scale government intervention in the economy for (and for the first time) explicitly economic objectives. This was then followed by the Second World War, in which governments assumed even greater powers of economic direction and control in order to wage the war, powers which they were reluctant to abandon once the war was over.

But even before that, the twentieth century had been marked on the left by the rise of socialism, and on the right by that of corporatist nationalism. Everywhere economic liberalism was in retreat. Just as the individualism of the eighteenth century provided the ethos of the United States, so the collectivism of the twentieth century provided the ethos of the Soviet Union. In Britain even a liberal like Keynes had, by 1930, come to the conclusion that the capitalist free-market economy was unacceptably wayward and flawed, and in particular had an inbuilt bias to underconsumption, recession and high and rising unemployment. The state, he believed, must therefore actively intervene in the economy, but not through the nostrums of the collectivists and detailed state intervention in decision making, to which he was resolutely opposed. Instead it should seek to maintain aggregate demand in the economy, which would otherwise be gravely deficient, by programmes of public works, leaving individuals to take their own decisions within that framework.

The Return of Economic Liberalism

But now there has been a further change. Over the last twenty years of the twentieth century, pretty well throughout the world, economic liberalism has made a comeback. The retreat of the state is better seen as the advance, once again, of economic liberalism. And while the most conspicuous aspect of this retreat is a retreat from collectivist interventionism, there is also growing and justified scepticism of the Keynesian alternative. During the rest of this chapter I shall be discussing why economic liberalism has made this comeback, what the consequences have been, and in particular, in the light of the financial turmoil now afflicting so much of the world, whether it is likely to last. Before I do this, however, it is important to be clear that economic liberalism, far from being a form of anarchism, assigns a very important economic role to the state. In part this stems from the fundamental pre-economic role of the state in setting and enforcing a proper legal framework, both in terms of criminal law – the maintenance of order – and civil law – the settlement of disputes. Far from being akin to the law of the jungle, with the devil taking the hindmost, an efficient and well-functioning market economy can exist only on the basis of the rule of law, both criminal and civil. It cannot work, for example, if competitors can be gunned down with impunity, if contracts are not enforceable in the courts, or if property rights are not similarly underpinned.

Alongside this, the state has a more explicitly economic role. The essence of the retreat of the state is the retreat from coercion, to a situation in which economic relations are a voluntary activity. But coercion can be exercised by others than the state. Thus it is part of the duty of the state to allow economic freedom to flourish by outlawing slavery and curbing the powers of monopolies and trade unions. It is also, of course, the role of the state to negotiate with other states – through the World Trade Organization, the former General Agreement on Tariffs and Trade (GATT), and in other ways

– a framework of rules to allow free trade. Finally, it is the duty of the state to provide a stable currency. So the retreat of the state from all-pervasive economic role it arrogated to itself throughout much of the twentieth century emphatically does not imply the unimportance of the state to the free economy. Far from it.

Reasons for its Return

Why, then, has this retreat of the state occurred? Why has economic liberalism made this largely unforeseen comeback? I do not believe it has anything to do with anything so trivial as the pendulum of economic fashion, or for that matter with the teachings of new gurus. Economic liberalism is, after all, not a new idea. Instead, it is a well-founded old theory that was temporarily, for the reasons I have indicated, in disrepute. Rather the retreat has happened, essentially, for three reasons. The first, and by far the most important reason, was that the twentieth-century experiment with big, interventionist, government turned out at best to be a severe disappointment, and at worst a major disaster. The second reason was the advent (partly as a result of the remarkable developments in information and communications technology) of what has come to be known as globalization: that is, the creation for many purposes of a single world market and world economy, in which physical distance is irrelevant. Globalization has not compelled the state to retreat, but it has made it harder for the state to impose its will, and forced it to pay a higher price should it seek to do so. The third reason was the emergence in the West of a number of political leaders – most notably Thatcher and her colleagues in Britain and the Reagan administrations in the United States – but we should not ignore the Labour government that came to power in New Zealand in the mid-1980s, who were resolutely opposed to collectivism and prepared to risk unpopularity to see their policies put into effect. So political leadership *does* matter.

However, to repeat, far and away the most important of these three reasons was the first. The twentieth-century experiment in state economic direction and intervention began, as we have seen, as a reaction to perceived market failure. But failure through government intervention proved to be far worse. The possibility that this might be so was foreseen right at the beginning of the advance of the state into economic management. Thus the eminent English economist Pigou, writing in 1920, warned:

> In any industry, where there is reason to believe that the free play of self-interest will cause an amount of resources to be invested different from the amount that is required in the best interests of the national dividend, there is a *prima facie* case for public intervention. The case, however, cannot become more than a *prima facie* one, until we have considered the qualifications which governmental agencies may be expected to possess for intervening advantageously. It is not sufficient to contrast the imperfect adjustments of unfettered private enterprise with the best adjustments that economists in their studies can

imagine. For we cannot expect that any public authority will attain, or even whole-heartedly seek, that idea. Such authorities are liable alike to ignorance, to sectional pressure and to personal corruption by private interest.[3]

Even so, after the traumatic experience of the world slump of the early 1930s, warnings such as this came to be brushed aside.

In 1998, in the light of the bitter lessons of the economic history of the twentieth century, we know better. The most telling lesson of all was provided by the collapse of communism in the Soviet Empire, and indeed the collapse of the Soviet Union and the Soviet Empire themselves, less than a decade ago. Here, after all, was the most thoroughgoing practical experiment in state economic control ever attempted. It was to collapse, completely, within the space of a single human lifespan, not as the result of war or violent revolution, but as a consequence of its total economic failure. Indeed, it was only after the collapse, when much that had hitherto been largely hidden from the rest of the world was revealed, that the unimaginably massive extent of that economic failure became fully apparent. History provides few better approximations to a controlled laboratory experiment than the experience of one country, Germany, artificially divided in two, with one economic system on one side of the divide and one on the other. Or look, again, at Asia. Despite the current turmoil (and I will return to that) it is, I believe, indisputable that those Asian countries – notably of course Japan, but equally Hong Kong and Singapore – that to a greater or lesser extent embraced the market economy and economic liberalism, have proved more successful and more prosperous than those – such as India and mainland China – which, until very recently, chose the collectivist, statist, approach. If there is anything we in Britain need to feel guilty about in our relations with our former dominions and colonies in Africa and Asia, it is not the largely beneficent nature of British imperial rule but the propagation, to their great cost, of collectivist, statist, economic doctrines by academics from the London School of Economics and their like-minded colleagues.

And what of the West, where the state also undoubtedly advanced in the economic sphere during the course of the twentieth century, albeit to a much less far-reaching extent than either in the Soviet Empire or the Third World? Here again, it is inescapable that the most successful, strongest, most vigorous and self-renewing economy has proved to be that of the United States, where the advance of the state in the economic sphere was most limited. Similarly one might focus on the situation in Britain, where for many years a substantial state-owned sector of the economy operated side by side with the private sector. For all the shortcomings of private enterprise in Britain, it became increasingly difficult to see the nationalized industries, as had initially been hoped by their creators, as shining examples of efficiency and service to the consumer. So the lesson of experience is clear. Pigou's 1920 warning was well founded. In the event, government failure has proved to be considerably more damaging than market failure.

But we should not be surprised at this. The central fact of life is that we are all fallible; we all make mistakes and will always do so. Markets make mistakes, and so do governments. Businessmen make mistakes, and so do politicians and bureaucrats. Thus the attempt to construct an economic system which will eliminate mistakes is doomed to failure. All we can sensibly do is to put in place a system in which mistakes are soonest recognized and most rapidly corrected. Whether in a despotism or a democracy, there is nothing harder for the state to admit than its mistakes, and no mistakes take longer to correct.

But it is not just detailed state intervention, in what Keynes called the 'interstices of the economy', and collectivism generally that has failed. The Keynesian alternative, to which I referred earlier, has also proved to be a false trail. In the first place, of course, the underlying diagnosis proved to be wrong. So far from having an inbuilt tendency to underconsumption and semi-slump, as Keynes believed, the democratic capitalist market economy has most of the time demonstrated in practice a bias in the direction of overconsumption and inflation. Of course, over the short term the economy advances not in a straight line but in a series of cycles of alternate boom and recession, which undoubtedly cause problems; latter-day Keynesians have seen it as the main economic task of government to iron out these cycles – this was the so-called stabilization policy. It may be that even this objective is misguided, and that the short-term cycle is in fact an agent of long-term growth, through the process of what Schumpeter called 'creative destruction'.

But all this is largely immaterial, since experience shows clearly that the cycle is ineradicable. One practical reason for this is that government (or central bank) measures, whether fiscal or monetary, cannot have an instantaneous effect, but operate – to the extent that they operate at all – only after a considerable time lag; and, since this is so, for a short-term stabilization policy to be a practical proposition, it has first to be possible to make reasonably accurate short-term economic forecasts. The lesson of experience, which has been subjected to the most careful academic scrutiny and analysis, is that this simply cannot be done, and happens only very infrequently by a fortunate accident. Indeed, more recently, academics using an esoteric mathematical technique known as 'non-linear signal processing analysis', which I certainly do not begin to understand, claim to have demonstrated that the nature of economic data is such that short-term forecasting is impossible. But I am not at all surprised. Keynes himself explained the origin of economic cycles very lucidly. It was, he claimed in the *General Theory*,[4] although this was dressed up in pseudo-scientific language, a result of changes in people's expectations. The notion that anything as psychological and subjective as people's expectations can be accurately forecast and calibrated is plainly absurd. In any event, the record of short-term forecasters speaks for itself.

So, to repeat, the short-term cycle is ineradicable, and outwith government control – although that does not stop the public and the media widely and erroneously believing that every twist and turn can be attributed to government policy. It is ironic that, if President Clinton remains in office, it will be largely because the American people believe that, despite his low crimes and misdemeanours, he has been a good president; and the reason they believe this is because they have been enjoying the fruits of a prolonged cyclical economic upswing which in fact is nothing whatever to do with him. Be that as it may, Keynesian economic policies have never worked in practice anywhere, at any time. Britain emerged, more quickly and more strongly than most countries, from the depression of the early 1930s not on the basis of Keynesian economics, which was ignored by governments at the time and implemented only after the war, but on the basis of cheap money and a series of rigorously balanced budgets. More recently, the attempt to find a Keynesian solution to the collapse of confidence and prolonged recession in Japan has proved completely unavailing. The practical result of the adoption of Keynesian stabilization policies over a number of years has (apart from the unfortunate miseducation of the public by politicians and economists alike) largely been that those countries that have adopted them have found themselves, at the end of the day, with higher levels of public spending, public deficits and taxation than they are comfortable with – and, when they have resorted to printing money rather than raising it by taxation, higher levels of inflation, too.

But the more lasting mischief done by the unthinking acceptance of Keynesianism in the West has been the emphasis it has placed, as Hayek, Keynes's greatest critic (whose criticisms proved to be fully justified), long ago pointed out, on macroeconomics rather than microeconomics, on the chimera of short-term aggregate stabilization, rather than what should be the true concern of economic policy makers, which is, to use Adam Smith's words, the 'nature and causes of the wealth of nations'. It has been the manifest failure, in these terms, of the twentieth-century experiment in big interventionist government that has been the principal cause of the retreat of the state, and the renewal of economic liberalism, over the last twenty years of the twentieth century.

The Consequences of Economic Liberalism

What have the consequences been? It is undoubtedly true that there is a conflict between freedom and security, and also between freedom and equality; and at the end of the day a choice has always to be made. It also true, however, that a prosperous nation can best afford to assist those who suffer most from poverty or insecurity, and should certainly do so. Until recently, most fair-minded observers must surely have been favourably impressed. In Britain, the performance of the privatized industries has far surpassed that of the nationalized industries they once were; the dragon of inflation has been slain; and lower tax rates, a significant part of the liberal economic agenda, have brought about a new dynamism. So great has the change been that we now have a Labour Prime Minister who claims to be New Labour, having jettisoned socialist economics completely, in conscious imitation of President Clinton, who presented himself as a New Democrat, opposed to the old ideas of big government and tax-and-spend. The United States, too, during the 1980s and 1990s, has achieved a remarkable economic renewal, even if claims about the so-called new paradigm are, to borrow from the admirable Alan Greenspan, 'somewhat over-exuberant'. Again, the countries of Central Europe – although clearly not Russia itself – have made remark-able economic progress since emancipating themselves from communist state control and embracing the market economy.

Until the late 1990s, however, the most outstanding success story for the market economy, over the previous couple of decades, looked to be the astonishing develop-ment of the so-called 'tiger economies' of the Far East – what even the staid World Bank was to describe, in the title of a study produced in 1993 as 'the East Asian economic miracle'. Today the tigers are in great distress: Russia is regressing to renewed state control, albeit not as thoroughgoing as before, and world financial markets are in a fair degree of turmoil, bringing down, *inter alia*, one of the biggest so-called hedge funds, which potentially threatening consequences to the banking system. The world's second largest economy, Japan, is mired in a deepening recession, and the prospect of a serious world recession, if not depression, is once again being voiced. Does all this mean that the retreat of the state in the economic sphere over the last twenty years of the twentieth century has been a great mistake, or at the very least that it has gone too far?

I do not believe that it does. If we look more closely at the facts, they suggest otherwise. In the former communist world, it is Russia, which reformed least, which has run into the greatest difficulties, and not the former satellite countries of Central Europe, which reformed most. Again, the Asian economies that are suffering most are those which proclaimed most stridently that they had discovered a 'third way', the so-called Asian model, in which the transition to free-market capitalism and economic liberalism (although, be it noted, seldom much political liberalism) was accompanied by a considerable degree of continuing government direction and control. This last policy was justified by the claim that wise governments could be counted on to take a long-term view of the countries' interests, in contrast to the alleged pathological short-termism of the markets; and there were many in the West who were all too ready to accept this. In fact, this alleged long-term view largely consisted of promoting massive uneconomic investment projects, usually owned by the president's friends and relations (so-called crony capitalism), and financed by banks which were leant on to do so by the power of the state and which were themselves inadequately financed, something hidden by deliberate lack of transparency and inadequate prudential regulation. And taking a global view, it is quite clearly those parts of the world economy, the United States and Europe, accounting for some 60 per cent of the total world economy, where economic liberalism is most deeply entrenched, that are proving the most economically robust during the current blizzard.

The Retreat of the State in Economic Management

The Question of its Permanence

But while short-term stabilization is, as I have already observed, a chimera, the capacity to avoid financial collapse is not. The governments and above all the central banks of the West have the means to avoid such a collapse, and they need to stand ready to use them. What is quite clear is that a new phase of protectionism and state intervention and control is no part of the remedy. My principal worry at the end of this century, I have to confess, concerns continental Europe. Not only does it appear somewhat complacently obsessed with the creation of the Euro and Economic and Monetary Union (EMU), at the expense of wider and more pressing issues, but its approach to economic liberalism has always been much more equivocal than in the Anglo-Saxon world; it is much more likely, therefore, to be tempted to respond to the current turmoil, when it does respond, in the wrong way. This has much less to do with the recent election of a red–green coalition in Germany than with what might be termed the 'Colbertian tendency' in France. Writing during the Second World War, towards the end of his classic and in many ways prophetic polemic *The Road to Serfdom*,[5] Hayek expressed interest in the idea of a European federation, on the grounds that, while national governments felt competent to plan their national economies, no federal European government could possibly be so stupid as to try and plan an economy as large, varied and diverse as that of Europe. I fear he underestimated the hubris of succeeding generations. In *Capitalisme contre*

Capitalisme,[6] a much more recent polemic almost as influential in France as Hayek's was in Britain, Michel Albert argues for a European federation explicitly on the grounds that in the modern world of the Anglo-Saxon global market economy and giant multinational corporations, only a European federal government would be big enough and strong enough to plan a European social market economy. There is a risk that this dangerous delusion, already influential in continental Europe, will gain much more support in the light of the current financial turmoil.

In Britain the danger is a different one. Here there is a much less élitist polity, and in that sense much more democratic than France: that is, in Britain public opinion matters. And it is striking that, although there is no mass public support for socialism as such in Britain, there is no mass public support for liberal economics either. In Britain, the prevailing instinct favours the popular fallacies of what David Henderson, in his brilliant Reith Lectures in 1985, somewhat dismissively called 'do-it-yourself economics'. As he puts it in an outstanding book published in 1998, do-it-yourself economics:

> holds for example that products, industries and activities can be characterised as 'essential' and 'non-essential', or ranked in order of priority, independently of willingness to pay at the margin; that national self-sufficiency in essentials is a key objective, which governments are responsible for achieving; that when transactions take place across national boun-

daries, the state is necessarily involved, so that international economic competition is predominantly between states; that exports represent a gain to each country, and imports a loss; that bilateral trade balances between countries are rightly matters of concern and official action; that tariffs, import restrictions and export subsidies serve to increase total employment; that administrative action to reduce or constrain the size of the labour force – such as compulsory reductions in working hours, enforced early retirement, or tighter restrictions on immigration – are bound to ease the problem of unemployment; that actions undertaken for profit, or more broadly from self-interest, are open to question as such; that when markets appear not to function well, the remedy lies with direct regulation; that market processes are often, if not inherently chaotic, disruptive and unjust; and that the responsibility for ensuring just and effective outcomes, over a vast range of particular cases, rests with governments. All this [Henderson observes] makes for an indefinitely large regulatory agenda.[7]

The prevalence of these views also underlines the democratic fragility of the retreat of the state over the past twenty years, despite its worldwide nature and marked overall success, a fragility which, as I have suggested, is particularly dangerous now, at the end of the twentieth century. Yet the dangers facing the world economy today are far less than in the 1930s, and we know from that experience the mistakes to avoid today. We know, too, that it was not the terminal crisis of capitalism that so many then thought; we further know how it was that the West successfully emerged from the slump of the 1930s. Above all, we know what a disappointment – and in some cases disaster – the twentieth-century experiment with big government and the interventionist state turned out to be in the economic sphere. Having, at long last, and with great difficulty, reversed the process, I cannot believe that our leaders will be so foolish as to repeat that failed experiment in the new century that is now upon us.

Notes

1. Adam Smith, *An Inquiry into the Nature and Causes of the Wealth of Nations*, Edinburgh, 1776.
2. Charles Darwin, *On the Origin of Species by means of Natural Selection, or the Preservation of Favoured Races in the Struggle for Life*, London, 1859.
3. Arthur C. Pigou, *The Economics of Welfare*, London, Macmillan, 1920, pp 331–2 of a later edition (cited by Henderson, p 76 and n 83; see note 7 below).
4. John Maynard Keynes, *The General Theory of Employment, Interest and Money*, London, Macmillan, 1936.
5. F. A. Hayek, *The Road to Serfdom*, London, Routledge, 1944.
6. Michel Albert, *Capitalisme contre Capitalisme*, Paris, Editions du Seuil, 1991.
7. David Henderson, *The Changing Fortunes of Economic Liberalism: Yesterday, Today and Tomorrow*, London, Institute of Economic Affairs, 1998, p 83.

The Retreat of the State in Social Welfare

ARTHUR SELDON

The Nature of the State

We live in a decisive stage in the history of the functions of government, in the liberties of the people, and in the nature of our democracy. All three are involved in the belated but growing acceptance in all schools of thought that the state must retreat from the over-expansion of government. Accelerating scientific and technological advances are more far-reaching in their economic and political repercussions than any since the Industrial Revolution of two centuries ago. They require us to question the powers of government and the political process that elects it. Not least must we consider that the state *should* do, but more what it now *can* do (and therefore what it *cannot* do) because of fundamental changes in everyday life. Here is the missing link in the efforts and failure of recent governments to adjust their welfare policies to changing conditions in society, conditions which are enhancing the power of the people to choose the lives they would like to, and now increasingly can, live.

The state is reluctant to accept both the weakening of its powers and the realization of its defects. In spite of its claims to do for the people better than they can do for themselves, the state is not all-seeing, impartial between supplicants for its favours, and efficient in the use of its revenue or borrowings. Furthermore it is not always just: it is tempted to yield to the strongest importunists, and not to the most deserving causes. It yields to people organized as producers much more than to the same people unorganized as consumers. It distorts their preferences by encouraging them to put their immediate short-term interests before their underlying long-term futures. In 1986, while on a visit to the site of the Battle of Gettysburg, in company with one American and one British economist working on the nature of democracy, we stood near the spot where in 1863 Abraham Lincoln promised government of, by, and for the people. Sadly the democratic state has emerged very differently from what Lincoln promised. In real life it has produced government 'of' the politically active, 'by' the political managers, 'for' the political importunists. In plain English, this is government of the busy, by the bossy, for the bully.

These excesses of the democratic state have provoked even more fundamental reactions from the people. It is the people who can now, and will increasingly in the coming years, limit the state's powers. The most recent developments in the distribution of power between government and governed are even more fundamental than Lincoln could have foreseen. In our times, today and tomorrow, and even more in the days and months and years after tomorrow, the state will gradually lose its powers. It has no magic wand. It cannot do what its wisest counsellors advise by passing laws, announcing rules, and proclaiming regulations. It has new and advancing competitors for its services, and they have been expanding and advancing to the point at which they are increasingly preferred. The waning power of the state, too long misunderstood by historians, is now more manifest, and especially in the realm of social welfare. The state has retuned its engines of expansion into state education, state medicine, state housing (through local government), state pensions, and state 'social' insurance since the Second World War and earlier. Indeed it has been better at tuning engines for advance than for the more relevant and more urgently needed tuning of engines for retreat.

The state is now in no man's land. It has advanced too far and cannot easily retreat in good order because it simultaneously risks unpopularity from the customary beneficiaries of its 'free' services, and growing reluctance to supply the resources for the people who want, and can find, better services elsewhere. In recent years democratic government has been intensively analysed by new schools of social scientists who reveal the decisions of the people's 'representatives' in government to be very different from those of the people themselves. This was true in the creation and post-war expansion of the welfare state, and now still more true in the failure to adapt the welfare state to a changing world. After a century or more of advance the state is facing unexpected obstacles to retreat. It is having to accept that its government is not sovereign or as final as it thought. Its overexpanding laws, rules and regulations can increasingly be escaped by the people.

Government has been slow to learn that the changing nature of economic life has increasingly put the preferences of the people beyond its own power to suppress those same preferences. And its statistics are misleading because more economic life lies beyond its reach; statistics of national production and incomes are inaccurate. They understate the total production of goods and services and overstate the degrees of poverty, inequality, and unemployment. All these historic trends underlie the unavoidably accelerating retreat of the state from social welfare that will continue to accelerate in the twenty-first century.

The explanations of the imperative task to adjust the domain of government to the increasing power of the people are economic, political, and technological. Above all they are economic, because the science of economics provides the unique indicator – costs and prices – of the most dispensable alternatives in deciding the best use of scarce resources. The welfare state has suffered from the crucial weakness that it has deprived itself of this instrument. Its claim to provide welfare 'free' was never well founded. Yet this truth was rarely questioned because, from the earliest days in the late nineteenth century, most people have paid for 'free' social welfare indirectly through taxes on purchases or earnings. Oscar Wilde's taunt in *Lady Windermere's Fan* that people who know the price of everything know the value of nothing was the opposite of the truth. It is still exploited by influential people who claim the common people's money to pay for their favoured causes – in the arts, heritage, environment and elsewhere. Their claim that the money they exact from government will do untold good is shallow. The so-called cultural 'values' of the cognoscenti are the preferences or prejudices of the few hundreds with influence in government; the people's money is questionably commandeered and misused by government. Lloyd George was condemned for 'raiding the Road Fund' for other purposes urgently required by government; the Lottery Fund is now being 'raided' for purposes not preferred by the people who risk their weekly pounds.

Only the 'empowerment' of the people by returning their purchasing power and through the freeing of prices will reveal the true preferences on which they would wish to spend their money. History suggests that they would be spending more on education, medical care, housing, and insurance and saving for the years after work than the state can now raise in taxes to spend *for them*. The concealing of these costs underlies the confused thinking in the retreat from social welfare. In its latest efforts to withdraw from some forms of social welfare the state confronts a new dilemma which stands midway between over-expansion and inability to retreat.[1]

Democracy has expanded all its four main functions: in social welfare, in the supply of the 'public' goods of law and order once thought the necessary function of government, in the public 'utilities' of fuel and transport, and in local government services (from providing literature for the working man to improve himself, to the tennis courts, swimming pools and golf courses – subsidized but not widely used by people too old to swim, too slow for tennis or too frail for golf). In all four functions, government has expanded too far into overgovernment. Its resources fall short of its capacity to supply the people with social services – in education, medical care, and housing; these same people increasingly obtain them from elsewhere at lower cost and higher quality. If government does not withdraw, that is, retreat unilaterally, it will lose both its authority to influence the pace of withdrawal and, even more fundamentally, weaken its repute within Lincolnian democracy as answerable to the people.

The Social Welfare Services Ripe for Withdrawal

The main elements of state welfare and its defective financing fall into three groups:

- *education and medical care* universally supplied and largely 'free' of direct payment at the time of service, but paid for indirectly by taxes;
- *housing* for five million families subsidized by low rents, and *minimum incomes* for all in sickness, unemployment or old age, and subsidized by disguised National Insurance costs;
- *discretionary 'charitable' assistance* supplied by general tax-paid subsidies.

The Retreat of the State in Social Welfare

The conventional historians of the social services assess the strengths and weakness of past government policies but draw unfounded conclusions which argue for further state activity to remove blunders or to extend measures that earlier proved ineffective. To such academics the costs of the social services to the nation are seen only as the financial outlays required for improvements. That approach is not sufficient to decide the best possible services for the people. The economist uses the 'counterfactual' approach which considers what other methods of organizing social welfare might historically have replaced the failed constructions of the state. These are the alternative forms of welfare that might have been organized in other ways than by government (central or local) but which have been lost for decades. This more revealing approach issued from the teaching of 'opportunity costs' by the Austrian School of Economics, led by Frederick Hayek who brought it to the London School of Economics in the 1930s. This school taught that the real 'costs' of the state, not least in welfare, were the alternatives that might have developed had they not been discouraged or suppressed by the state. This vital missing link in its social welfare policies has long been neglected by the British state. What the state should have discovered after the Second World War, or before it, were the alternatives lost for far too long, the opportunities forgone by the persistence of the state in suppressing services that had long before emerged spontaneously in the early, mid- or late nineteenth century. These lost alternatives emerged from the natural growing instinct of people in families to take care of their own, throughout all the vicissitudes of life.

But instead the British family has been weakened because the state has usurped the authority of parents. Few children, especially in the lower-income families, have looked to their parents to provide their schooling, their medical care, or even their homes. They have had to look to the political authorities, the politicians and their 'public' servants, who have widened their powers to invade family bonds. The 'opportunity cost' approach reveals the long-ignored loss of another virtue of the people. In the perspective of history it is now clear that the state discouraged or suppressed spontaneous assistance to friends, neighbours and strangers by the personal charity that would have developed through the churches or through local groups of citizens; this is the selfless humanity that has long grown on a much larger scale in that other England that developed in the United States of America. It is not surprising that economists rather than sociologists, impressed by the powers of the state, have argued that the church encourages good relationships with non-churchgoers as well as churchgoers; in this they have followed their founder, Adam Smith. An economist in the USA has recently discovered[2] that, where state subsidies ceased, church membership and the demand for preachers rose markedly. Churches prospered when church leaders had to appeal to individual worshippers for encouragement and support rather than to legislators in government. Individual people as members of cohesive families were more sensitive to the condition of the less fortunate than they were as taxpayers.

As the state inevitably retreats in the twenty-first century we may expect the natural instinct of humanity, the urge to help the unfortunate, to expand with rising incomes. The efforts of the churches in founding schools for the young, supporting hospitals for all ages, building almshouses for the old, and giving money and comfort to the poor will grow far beyond the capacity of the state to supply these things from taxes unwillingly paid. Small wonder that parents in all social classes have usually preferred their children to attend church schools, rather than secular schools subject to political control by local authorities; Mr and Mrs Blair typify many other British parents. The difference is that working-class parents anxious about lagging children do not have the cultural influence of middle-class people to make their case with head teachers, hospital officials, housing managers, or National Insurance officials for better or early consideration. They also lack the power to escape from lagging secular schools by using the voucher method, a system which the government has abandoned in Britain for nursery schools, but which is showing how it can widen choice for working-class families in several states of the USA, where it is welcomed by lower-income black parents.

Arthur Seldon

The Rejection of State Welfare

The main reasons why individuals and families are now rejecting state welfare and withdrawing increasingly from state services are four-fold: first, rising incomes; second, technological advances; third, the reluctance to pay for state services through charges, insurance or taxes; and fourth, the widening number of escapes offered through informal employment, barter, electronic money, or by purchase from competing private suppliers at home and overseas.

Rising Incomes

Rising incomes are enabling more families across the income scale to pay for schooling by fees, for medical care by insurance, for housing by purchase, and for pensions and loss of income in sickness and unemployment again by insurance and saving in various forms.

Technological Advances

Personal and family withdrawal from state services is expedited by the technological advances that enable industry to produce 'bespoke' goods and services tailored for individual and family requirements in place of standardized state service 'off the peg'. It must have been apparent to the well-intentioned supporters of 'social' welfare (especially after the Second World War) that the standardized state services would before long be rejected. They mostly provide 'straightjacket' schooling and medicine, standardized homes and uniform pensions. Yet millions of people of all ages and incomes increasingly cook (or buy) individually created meals, wear individually tailored clothes, live in homes built in varying shapes and sizes, filled with the latest labour-saving devices (and leisure amenities for discriminating homeowners) and accumulate pensions for people retiring not at the state's artificial ages of 60 or 65 but at varying ages from 55 to 75 – or even 85.

Reluctance to Pay for State Services

The retreat by the people, if not by the state, from social welfare is increasingly stimulated by the reluctance of the beneficiaries to pay for it in the only ways they can – by charges, insurance or taxes. The increasing resistance to higher taxes takes the form of both legal avoidance and illegal evasion. They are legally separate but functionally linked and morally difficult to distinguish between. They are linked because increasing experience of tax avoidance teaches new methods of tax evasion. They are legally separate but recent Chancellors of the Exchequer in 1997 and 1998 have revealed a reluctance or inability to separate the two. Their plight in financing government is indicated by the self-contradictory anxiety of successive Chancellors to penalize as illegal the tax avoidance that the law specifically allows as legal for the intention of earners of all kinds of income – wages, salaries, fees, commissions, 'tips', and profits to minimize their loss of earnings by taxes by varying their working lives. This is evidence of the desperation and increasing hostility of an impecunious British government to its historically law-abiding citizens. Its excessive requirement for revenue to finance services that taxpayers are evidently reluctant to use and pay for is weakening the bonds of mutual trust that should underlie a democratic government which spends over 40 per cent of national income on such services.

The latest evidence of government desperation is the 'psychological warfare' waged against the generality of the profession of accountants on whom the Inland Revenue depends to present taxpayers' accounts. There is here a new moral dilemma for government that will drive it to retreat further from social welfare and to leave taxpayers to pay for private services they prefer by methods they prefer. If the state is indeed driven to penalize taxpayers for acts that are legal it will further risk resistance to other laws, rules and regulations over the whole range of economic life. It is a long time since the peasants of Kent (where I live) rose in 1381 to rebel against their taxes. But now I hear the rumblings of rebellion in the most bourgeois of churchgoing Kentish homes. The question must now be faced: we need to decide where the essential blame lies – with the taxers who demand more in revenue than the people are readily prepared to pay – or with the taxpayers for rejecting taxes seen as impertinently invasive of family and working lives.

There is now increasing research by economists into the extent and likely reasons for the intertwined combination of avoidance and evasion that I have christened 'tax avoision'. It is no longer sufficient to continue with

labels that beg the question of the relative moral responsibility of the citizen and the state implied by the
old term 'black market' or by the 'underground' that
echoes the wartime resistance of the French to oppres-
sion and tyranny. I use the morally neutral term 'parallel
economy' as the truest description of the loss of sympathy between government and people. And the avoidance of moral condemnation offers the best hope of
returning harmony by arranging taxes that people will
willingly pay for goods and services they cannot buy in
open markets. The best researches of the extent and
reasons for tax rejection have lately revealed that it is
essentially the excesses of government that have
depressed tax revenues.[3]

It is no longer true, as it may once have been in the
days of the smugglers and lately of the drug peddlers
(and is still stubbornly asserted by government
spokesmen and civil servants), that the sole or main way
to maintain tax revenue is to raise tax rates. The most
refined researches, by Professor Friedrich Schneider of
the Johannes Keppler University in Austria, reveal that
tax revenues are depressed essentially by four causes:
increases in direct taxes on incomes, indirect taxes on
purchases, the complexities of the taxation structure as
a whole, and the severity of the regulation of industry
and economic life in general. What is true in Austria is
probably true, partly or largely, of Britain. In its search
for finance to pay for the social welfare system, remain-
ing after a too reluctant retreat by the state, the British
government now would be wise to conduct similar
researches.

Arthur Seldon

Methods of Avoidance

The fourth reason for government to retreat from social
welfare comprises the increasing and developing escapes
to new sources of goods and services from national and
overseas suppliers brought to every private home by the
Internet. There is much to be said about all the rapidly
accelerating developments that ease 'escapes' from
government; I settle on barter as the most natural but
most neglected escape. Barter can enable otherwise law-
abiding citizens to exchange personal services produced
by specialized skills. As such it is designed essentially to
benefit friends, neighbours, members of clubs and other
associations in widening circles by producing non-
monetary 'incomes' nominally otherwise taxable. There
are no official statistics or estimates of this return to
natural exchange, but the informal evidence indicates
substantial development in recent years. This is
undoubtedly likely to form a rapidly increasing feature
of British private and communal life. The quiet grass-
roots revolution in the form of local exchange and trading systems (LETS) has been recorded by the press over
a period of several years. Most lately it has been docu-
mented by consistent research in England.[4] Such
exchanges can be seen as a new form of spontaneous
private welfare rescuing people with low incomes, or
no incomes at all, from avoidable poverty. The latest
development sees it lubricating barter exchange by
forms of local 'money'. Simple barter is difficult to
arrange because it requires a double coincidence of
wants: individuals must want precisely what other indi-

54

viduals offer. This pure exchange of barter is eased by a new kind of 'money' that satisfies its essential economic function as anything that is generally acceptable in exchange.

There was a time when barter meant the direct exchange of goods for other goods by specialists in complementary skills – for example, primitive farmers exchanging with hunters. In the 1990s or earlier, informal local currencies have been easing exchange between people of modest means through a modern form of what Samuel Smiles would have called 'Self-Help' in local exchange and trading systems. In West Norfolk, the new money is called 'shells'. In Greenwich the name is 'anchors', in Brixton 'bricks', and in Manchester and no doubt other former textile areas of the North West 'bobbins'.

In parts of Yorkshire a new currency is being used, in effect 'exchanged', for personal services – house maintenance, gardening, and childminding – and for everyday goods – food and (second-hand) clothing. Its use is being further extended to training or tuition in manual or artistic skills as in painting and cooking.

These are early forms of a new growth of informal exchanges in free markets that will liberate unused skills and create new forms of income. They illustrate the old truth, long forgotten, that the people have been misled to expect government to provide services they could better provide for themselves. In King's Lynn and West Norfolk the LETS have developed mutual aid by advice and assistance in everyday activities that encourage local communal life. The far-reaching potential of this spontaneous development is being harnessed by local authorities. The European Commission has incorporated the promotion of LETS into urban and regional development. The obstacle so far seems to be government in Whitehall. The uncertainty whether LETS earnings will count against social security benefits has discouraged participation by unemployed people. The Federal Government of Australia encourages such forms of exchange precisely as a new way to find work training and experience. The possibility of exonerating LETS from Whitehall rules might liberate many more people into dispensing with the state welfare for which they cannot or will not pay.

The Culpability of Overgovernment

The pioneering spirit of the English, which created the merchant venturers, the East India Company, and the entrepreneurial risk-taking spirit that prompted innovation in British industry, has not been conspicuous in the structures of the post-war government. These structures created the latest expansion in social services but there is now a reluctance to retreat in the face of economic change. The lack of a clear understanding of the imperatives of retreat is now revealed in the four divergent approaches to the belated reforms.

The Secretary of State for Education is at least willing to invite advice from people with experience of running the private schools that have transcended the defects of the state system and its schools: generally lower standards of performance, unruly behaviour including assault of teachers, and truancy. The difficulty remains of building advice services from private organizations. Moderate investors must be persuaded to risk their savings with schools sanctioned by central government and run by local officials with little knowledge of and less sympathy with the commercial skills required for the high efficiency demanded in competitive private schooling.

The Secretary of State for Health sees no flaws in a state system that has chronically failed to raise as much funding as healthcare systems in all other western countries in Europe, and even more in North America, where combinations of tax financing with optional private insurance raise far more – 35 percent more in Europe, 50 per cent in Australasia, 60 per cent in the USA – than in the British National Health Service (NHS). He is prepared to continue a fifty-year-old system unchanged on the same principles – no knowledge of costs – for a further fifty years. A century of the NHS which learns nothing from other countries would look sadly out of place in the likely world of the twenty-first century.

The government has no fundamental solution for improving the conditions in which five million elderly couples live out their years in *council housing* or highrise blocks. These long-outdated structures cannot be adapted to the much higher standards of private owners or tenants, not least among their own children. Government expedients include short-term increases in yet more subsidies to patch up council homes which will be of little interest to younger people as their new homes in

2010 or 2020; alongside this stands the latest drastic and desperate expedient of demolishing large numbers of council homes in the slums.

The fourth service, the unfunded 'pay-as-you-go' *National Insurance pension*, has finally been acknowledged as a failure that will not produce the higher incomes in retirement that most people have come to expect. The new proposal for a compulsorily funded private pension paid by insurance and invested to yield the income to pay the pensions is a confession of failure of statesmanship. It comes too late to save enough for the incomes that will be required in old age by those already over the age of fifty-five.

All these state services are destined to be perpetually short of the tax funds necessary to raise their standards. The only long-term solution is to recognize that they were created when tax revenue seemed secure. The ultimate solution in the twenty-first century is for the state to accept the necessity to retreat in good order by returning taxes to the parents, patients, tenants and pensioners to enable them to buy schools, hospitals, homes and pensions of their own choice on the open market. The sooner this ultimate retreat is arranged the more the state can help it to be orderly. If not, democracy will be seen to have no policies for an advancing society. Much of current revenue is required to repair existing social welfare buildings – schools, hospitals, housing, and offices. The essential flaw of contemporary democratic government is that it requires frequent but increasingly reluctant voter approval to maintain the good order of structures inherited from the past. Much the same is true of schools and hospitals, social 'homes' for the unruly young and the uncomfortable old, and the clerical offices that disfigure our towns, not least when they are newly built for the thousands of public officials who may not require them for much longer.

Most of these structures were built by government in the twentieth century; they now plague the government of today. It need no have been the fate of our children, the sick, working-class families, or the ageing if government had retreated from social welfare in the last hundred years as people built preferred services by paying fees, charges or prices. That is what they had been doing since the early nineteenth century until well into the twentieth. Little of that is taught in our school history books or discussed currently by sociologists. In 1860, the Newcastle Commission reported that three out of four working-class children were at schools charging fees paid for by their parents, sometimes aided by charities or the church.[5] After the establishment by Gladstone of local board schools in 1870, direct spending by families was increasingly replaced by indirect spending by the same people in their taxes on their purchases, but with much less influence on their schools.

Towards the last third of the nineteenth century, working men were insuring privately for medical care with friendly societies and similar working-class organizations.[6] In 1911 when the Liberals, Lloyd George and Winston Churchill, introduced compulsory social insurance for 11.5 million male employees no fewer than 9 million had been covered for some time by private insurance. Long before, in the 1870s and 1880s, working people in the industrial north were buying their homes with the help of the early building societies. And, in 1946 to 1948, when post-war Labour, sadly encumbered by pre-war thinking, introduced the enlarged pensions schemes, Attlee and his colleagues must have known that the occupational pensions begun in the 1930s were spreading and would have spread further. This was a failure of democratic government, not least in its short-term myopia induced by the anxiety to win voter gratitude by dealing with urgent, pressing, short-term 'problems' that build complex distortion of policies in the longer run. The social services demonstrate more than other policies the unsuitability of politics in education, medical care, housing, and much else that can damage family and private lives. With the best of intentions, but the worst of democratic foresight, governments down the decades have expanded social welfare too soon, too far, and too long, and their retreat is now too slow.

Admirers of Beveridge have persevered with the social schemes he outlined in 1942, some of which he had himself abandoned in his last years of disillusion with politicians. Meeting with him as early as 1947, as a fellow member of the Liberal Party, to discuss aspects of state pensions on which the Liberal Party had asked me to chair an enquiry, I found he was busy writing a book, *Voluntary Action*.[7] In this he warned uninformed enthusiasts that the 'social welfare' being prepared by the politicians would endanger the very institutions that had been built by 'the people', that is, by the lower-income working classes. In 1962, when two former

Fabian economists, the renowned Colin Clark and the sage Graham Hutton, joined me and my Institute of Economic Affairs colleague, Ralph (later Lord) Harris, to dine with Beveridge at the Reform Club, he lamented the fate of his national pension scheme. His saddest regret seemed to be the failure of perhaps the most upright academic-politician of the day, Hugh Gaitskell, to follow his advice and build the National Insurance Fund over twenty years, before paying the new retirement pensions. The political excuse was that the higher benefit could not be paid to other beneficiaries without including pensioners – another excuse for a short-term expedient that created long-term tensions *après le déluge*. The National Insurance Fund was for only a few years a 'Fund' invested to yield income for the pensioners. For most of the years since then it has been not a fund, but rather a tank with a pipe of National Insurance contributions *leading in* and a large pipe of pensions *leading out*. That is still true in 1998, with the added burden for people approaching pensionable age that they must – by government decree – personally accumulate a second pension. One other academically-responsible politician, Sir Keith Joseph, saw the coming dilemma in the 1970s, but his political friends did not share or support his anxious vision.

The Historic Delusion

Talk of 'the retreat of the state' creates apprehension among the many who have regarded it as the saviour of the sick and the poor. A dominant anxiety is that democracy has taught the doctrine of Thomas Hobbes that its creation of 'sovereignty' (government power over economic life) is essential for the maintenance of good order and civilized life. The alternative to the political state with the power to regular economic life and to coerce the people to conform to it, warned Hobbes, was 'a state of nature' that would create perpetual 'war of all against all' in which life would be 'nasty, brutish and short'. This dire prospect has habituated the Western world into accepting and tolerating the political state with its overgovernment. Yet from the start of the twentieth century or earlier overgovernment has been an obstruction to the liberties that democracy was supposed to protect.

Hobbes wrote in the seventeenth century. His warning has long been overtaken by the technological advances of the nineteenth century with its massive rises in living standards. A century after Hobbes, at the end of the eighteenth century, it was still plausible for Tom Paine to urge, in his classic *The Rights of Man*, an early structure of Beveridge Plan benefits from maternity grants through a form of cash school vouchers all the way to funeral expenses. In the introduction to the 1958 edition of *The Rights of Man* I wrote of Paine's proposals:

In his day this was advanced thinking. In our day we have no sooner erected a structure of state provision for the needy than it has in some respects become out of date with rising personal incomes. The welfare state is, or in a free society should be, a passing phase; but there is a danger that it will be erected into a permanent appendage: the crutch will be beaten into a shackle.[8]

So it has been for forty years since 1958, and indeed for over a century and a half. The recent reforms in state welfare call out of us a reassessment of Hobbes' flawed warning. This was rejected by the inter-war Labour-inclined scholar, A. D. Lindsay, the Master of Balliol, in his introduction to Hobbes' *Leviathan*: he argued that law is not obeyed solely because it is created by the state; rather it is respected essentially because it is wanted by the people. This truth is still overlooked by the politicians of our day.

> . . . if Hobbes is right [said Lindsay] in maintaining that without some authority there can be no state . . . he forgets that the power of the sovereign, even though legally unlimited, depends upon the skill with which it gives expression to the general will; if it disregards the general will there will come a point at which no amount of legal or constitutional machinery will avert disaster.[9]

The legal and constitutional machinery of the twentieth century has not prevented the emerging revolt of the masses or the remonstrances of the bourgeois.

Hobbes was earlier refuted by the seventeenth-century philosopher, Benedict de Spinoza, whose Portuguese family fled from persecution to Holland. Lindsay repeats Spinoza's magisterial dictum:

A sovereign has right insofar as he has might, and he
has might only insofar as he rules in such a way that
his subjects regard rebellion as a greater evil than
obedience.[10]

The sovereign state is now having to retreat from social
welfare and other superfluous functions. But it is
retreating too slowly. The subjects are rebelling. And
they will continue to rebel until government retreats
sufficiently to liberate the freedoms created by economic
advance.

Notes

1. A. Seldon, *The Dilemma of Democracy: the Political Economics
   of Over-Government*, Hobart Paper 136, London, Institute of
   Economic Affairs, 1998.
2. Professor Kelly Olds, 'Privatising the Church', *Journal of Political
   Economy* 102 (1994) pp 277–97.
3. Professor Friedrich Schneider, 'The Shadow Economies of
   Western Europe', *Economic Affairs*, 17, 3 (September 1997) pp
   42–8.
4. G. Seyfang and C. C. Williams, 'Give DIY Economics a Break:
   Local Exchange and Trading Systems Are a Great Benefit to the
   Unemployed', *New Statesman*, 27 March 1998, p 24.
5. Professor E. G. West, *Education and the State: a Study in Political
   Economy*, London, Institute of Economic Affairs, 1965.
6. Dr David Green, 'Medical Care without the State', in Arthur
   Seldon, ed, *Re-privatising Welfare: after the Lost Century*, IEA
   Readings 45, London, Institute of Economic Affairs, 1996, pp
   21–37.
7. Sir William Beveridge, *Voluntary Action: a Report on Methods
   of Social Advance*, London, Allen and Unwin, 1948.

8. Arthur Seldon's Introduction in Thomas Paine, *The Rights of Man*, Everyman's Library 718, J. M. Dent, 1906 reprinted with a new introduction 1958, pp v–xiii.
9. A. D. Lindsay's Introduction in Thomas Hobbes, *Leviathan*, Everyman's Library 691, J. M. Dent, 1924, pp vii–xxiv.
10. A. D. Lindsay in Thomas Hobbes, *Leviathan*, Everyman's Library 691, J. M. Dent, 1924, p xxiv.

The Retreat of the State from Overseas Development

MICHAEL TAYLOR

The British State: Retreat or Advance

My immediate reaction to this subject is that in 1998 it raises an issue which is long since dead. Five or ten years ago we might well have girded our loins to bemoan the retreat of the British state from overseas development and to resist it. Indeed many of us did just that by campaigning against aid and trade policies that did more to promote the trade of rich countries than benefit the poorer ones, and by demanding without much success a reversal in the decline of the aid budget.

But those days have gone. Thatcherism has been over-taken (or certainly overhauled) by New Labour and in the field of overseas development we are witnessing not the retreat of the state but its advance. The current Secretary of State for International Development – Clare Short – has a seat in the Cabinet. She has published a government White Paper on the subject – the first in over twenty years – called *Eliminating World Poverty: a Challenge for the 21st Century*.[1] She has secured an

66

increase in the development budget amidst all the talk of tight controls on spending. The government is committed to the International Development Targets to cut the worst of poverty in the world in half by 2015; there are tangible signs that it will play a leading role in cancelling the unpayable debts of the poorest countries by the millennium. It has a strategy for partnership in this great cause of poverty reduction with other governments, the private and voluntary sectors, and for reviving development education in schools and raising public awareness so that more and more people understand the issues and give their support to government action. The unwillingness of previous governments has been superseded by the political will of the government now in office. Retreat is not really on the agenda. It is a straw man.

Amidst all this euphoria, however, there is inevitably a feeling in some quarters that not all the moves are in the right direction, so maybe we should look at the issue a little more carefully before rushing to judgement. I want first to make clear what I mean by 'development' and look at the reasons why a state might retreat from it, whether it actually does so or not. Development is a big word touching on all aspects of our human life – material and spiritual, individual and social – but in this chapter we shall narrow its meaning to the provision of basic human needs, mainly of a material kind, without which any rounded human existence can hardly be sustained. People need food and drink, shelter, education and healthcare if they are to have any real chance of developing and being fulfilled. These basic provisions are not the finishing line of development but they are the necessary starting blocks. Such needs can be met in four main ways, none entirely discrete from the others. The first is by *emergency relief aid* in a situation like Southern Sudan or the recent floods in Bangladesh or the refugee camps of Rwanda or Kosovo. The second is by *service delivery* where schools and clinics and water are provided by established agencies such as the state or voluntary organizations. The third is by *development programmes* where poor people become actively involved in tackling their own problems. The fourth is by *political and economic reform* which seeks to change for the better the conditions which create and aggravate poverty. This can involve anything from debt relief and trade policies to promoting democracy, and can reach to the high politics of security and military intervention in situations of conflict. Here then are four areas within which the state may advance or retreat, becoming more or less actively involved and there seem to me to be five reasons for moving in one direction or the other.

The first is *ideological*. The move is motivated by a deeply held conviction likely to be called 'principled' if you approve of it and 'prejudiced' if you don't. The most famous of recent examples is Mrs Thatcher's dictum that 'there is no such thing as society'. Her conviction is the child of Protestant individualism. It regards the individual and his or her personal responsibility for themselves as the prime reality. Social relations are secondary. Self-help is everything. Dependency is viewed with horror and the biblical injunction – that 'we are members one of another' – with apparent incomprehension. The state as an expression of society, of mutual care and interdependency, is inevitably consigned to a minimalist role and the poor, as the object of development, are readily seen as the 'undeserving poor' who are unwilling to help themselves but must learn to do so and not for one minute receive the sort of aid and comfort which encourages them to lean back on others.

A second motive for retreat is less dogmatic. We might call it *strategic*. It is a judgement about which policies are likely to work. For example, if the aim is to create wealth and remove poverty, then it is far better to rely on the market than the interfering state. Being more competitive, private enterprise will be more efficient. Some will make more money in the process than others but all the boats will rise. The state should withdraw and leave the private sector to get on with the job.

This strategic motive comes close to a third which we might call *instrumental*. The state may believe in society and shared efforts to meet human need. It may agree with a certain strategy or policy but it may still judge that it is better implemented by agencies other than the state. It therefore withdraws for purely pragmatic reasons. An example would be emergency relief aid. The armed forces of the state have been involved on occasions, as in Bosnia for example, but in general it is best left to agencies like the United Nations (UN) or to the voluntary sector or again to private enterprise. A large exhibition was mounted in Geneva in 1996 under the title 'World Aid Inc'. It set out to argue that the private sector could deliver food, blankets and medicines to starving people more quickly and at less cost than anyone else. States these days are inclined to take the point, and not just about aid but across a whole range of services. They should be provided but it is not necessary or desirable for the state to provide them itself.

A fourth motive for retreat, besides the ideological, strategic and instrumental, is *incapacity*. Even if the state wishes to be involved it lacks the wherewithal to do so. This was the excuse put forward by earlier British governments for cutting the aid budget and moving away from, rather than even gradually towards, the famous UN target of 0.7 percent of Gross National Product (GNP). In hard times it simply could not afford to contribute any more. Now, however, the capacity and power of the nation state is challenged on a much bigger scale, as has been indicated in earlier chapters. During the summer of 1998 as interest rates remained stubbornly high, and jobs began to be cut and exports flag, business appealed to the government to 'do something about the economy'. The fact is that, with globalization, the liberalization of the market and the movement of capital, the blurring of national boundaries as goods cross them more freely, the lifting of tariffs, the rise of transnational corporations and the advent of information technology and communications, it is more than likely that business is better placed to do something about the economy than the state. Transactions worth over one trillion dollars take place every day on international exchange markets. Rapid computer calculation means that companies and speculators can evade national regulations. 'Financial derivatives' (which I don't pretend to understand) allow companies to buy protection against devaluation or changes in national interest rates. The state may wish to take the credit when the economy is going well, but in good times and in bad it has less control and is on the retreat. Insofar as the fundamental problems of poverty and underdevelopment can only be tackled by reformed economic systems, when the state retreats from economic power it retreats by the same token from development.

Finally the state may retreat for *democratic* reasons. One much discussed example has been 'compassion fatigue', and here the development lobby may at times have shot itself in the foot. It has been highly critical of some big, government-sponsored projects, including the Pergau Dam, but this may only have fuelled public suspicion that overseas aid is a waste of money. That suspicion tends to be confirmed by the sad spectacle of repeated disasters in countries like Sudan (from war) and Bangladesh (from floods). The voters are not so much weary of being compassionate as weary of seeing 'the taxpayers' money' being wasted. Governments already disinclined to fund aid and development can then appeal to the electorate for support or at least assume that it will not overcomplain if little is done. A government all set to engage in development will need to educate the electorate all over again if it is to enjoy democratic support.

The Retreat from the Northern NGOs

Let me now illustrate some of these points by turning to the area of the development debate which is most familiar to me (as a former Director of Christian Aid) where the Blair government, for all its renewed commitment to international development, can be experienced as 'retreating'. I refer to the relationship between the government (or the state) and British NGOs including Christian Aid, the Catholic Fund for Overseas Development (CAFOD), Oxfam, Save the Children, Action Aid and many others.

British NGOs have universally welcomed the government White Paper on development with its commitment to cut abject poverty in half by the year 2015. But they have an edgy relationship with the Department for International Development (DFID) and its Secretary of State and perceive the government as distancing itself from them instead of forging even closer relations. There is 'retreat' rather than 'advance'.

The government White Paper has much to say about 'partnerships'. Poverty cannot be tackled by the government alone. Its main partners in reaching the International Development Targets, for example, will be other governments; but it also intends to co-operate with Southern NGOs (and to fund them) and, when it comes to emergency relief, with the UN multilateral agencies. British NGOs have received considerable government funding in the past (though the balance of it has shifted from the British government itself to the European Union) for emergency relief, and for ongoing development work, but they are unlikely to receive so much in the future. This government is far less willing than the last to fund development projects and programmes and has already shown itself highly resistant to appeals for emergency aid. In the Sudan, for example, it first claimed that there was no real need and then preferred to fund the UN rather than British NGOs who eventually issued a joint emergency appeal. If all else fails and Southern governments are unwilling or incapable of co-operating then the DFID may turn to British NGOs as 'partners of last resort'. But their role will then be as contractors, carrying out government policies on government terms. The government is enthusiastic about working with British NGOs on two 'home' fronts. One is campaigning, for example on fair trade issues and the cancellation of unpayable international debts (though the NGOs and the Jubilee 2000 Campaign have not always seen eye to eye with the Minister on this subject), and the other is education and increasing public understanding and support for development.

The government's reasons for distancing itself from British NGOs are varied. Let me suggest five. *First* there may be a strong feeling that the NGOs are not the most efficient or reliable partners for carrying out emergency relief work. The argument here is 'instrumental' (about who does what best). NGOs have been criticized in recent years (following the Rwanda crisis, for example, when millions fled over the borders into Goma and elsewhere) for lack of co-ordination and even for competing between themselves. They have been accused of having a vested interest in emergencies. They hype up the numbers of people involved (this was specifically said of Rwanda, though the agencies were later proved right). They exaggerate the degree of suffering (this was specifically said of Sudan where the Blair government resisted the agencies' appeals for help, downplaying the need and arguing that the problem was political; though the agencies were later proved right). Agencies, it is said, put very little effort into dealing with underlying causes, like the politics of Central Africa, or into resolving the continuing conflict in Sudan; and all this because it serves their own institutional ends. They do other work but basically they need emergencies and the money and profile that come with them in order to stay in business.

Second there is a 'strategic' reason why the government distances itself from the traditional development work of NGOs. It is typically 'project' based. 'Projects' have only recently begun to give way to 'programmes'. A project may involved installing wells and water pipes in a number of villages, or helping farmers to regenerate land by terracing hillsides, or training local village health workers, or building low-cost housing, or supporting small income-generating projects or running informal literacy groups. Often such projects are a far cry from the ideal of 'integrated development' where not one but all of a community's interrelated needs are tackled together. Again these projects tend to be unco-ordinated, with one agency funding a project here and another one there, often with different approaches and, when it comes to proving to the donors back home that their money is being spent on good and interesting work, again in competition with one another. Yet again these localized attempts (which 'programmes' over wider areas are meant to improve) at transforming a poor region or country can be too small and too vulnerable and discrete to count. Projects falter as they are almost bound to do, given the difficulties. Agencies and their funding come and go. Overall the situation may change very little.

This leads to a *third* reason. Too often and especially when it comes to delivering basic services such as healthcare and education, NGOs are not the appropriate body. They try to do what governments should do. They are inevitably selective. Some communities get a hospital or a clinic and others don't. Some rural areas get a school and others are left without. The approach is patchy where it ought to be universal. (The criticism is an ironic echo for me of the criticism I and others often levelled at child sponsorship schemes. Inexorably they single out some children and leave others. Here NGOs are criticized for much the same mistake though in this case it is communities rather than children which are singled out for preferential treatment.) Furthermore, continue the critics, NGOs are not just a poor and patchy alternative to universal state provision. They can actually take over from national and local governments. They subvert the state. This complaint was voiced more than once by the government of Rwanda as it struggled to establish a grip on its country's affairs.

A *fourth* reason why the state has apparently retreated from its partnership with British NGOs relates to its concern to foster civil society and democracy and the participation of ordinary people in good governance especially in the South. Southern NGOs are part of civil society. Where they are funded by British NGOs the Northern NGOs are said to have an unfortunate effect. If the experience and expertise of the North is too much in evidence in a school or a hospital, for example, then the Southern NGO will take so much longer to gain experience and develop the expertise for itself. The North will perpetuate dependency rather than let go and allow Southern NGOs to stand on their feet.

A *fifth* and final reason for retreat is on the border between the ideological and the strategic. It may be at the root of the increasingly uneasy alliance between the British government and British NGOs for all the talk of partnership. The NGOs are seen as basically old-fashioned. They are essentially 'aid agencies' and aid belongs to the past. The NGOs are linked to an out-of-date approach which used to believe that aid and welfare handouts, charity and lady bountifuls, were the appropriate responses to poverty. In this government's opinion they most definitely are not. Not only do we need a structural approach to poverty which tackles its political and economic roots, but the poor themselves do not want our aid or welfare or charity. Like the rich they much prefer to stand on their own feet and look after themselves. They don't want aid but the opportunity to earn a living and make their own way in the world and care for themselves and their families. They don't want handouts. They want their rights, and having got them they will then accept the responsibilities that go with them. Aid and development agencies, all of them officially 'charities' under English law, do not sit easily with the contemporary approach to development and the policies of a Blairite government.

This fivefold 'retreat of the state' from the traditional British NGOs has nothing whatsoever to do with Mrs Thatcher's ideological disbelief in society and her consequent antipathy to the 'nanny' state. It has much more to do with strategy, appropriate instruments and agents for the job in hand, and the philosophy of 'opportunity not aid'. NGOs do not claim to be above criticism or the need to change but it would be quite unjust to leave the impression that they have nothing of any substance to say in reply to all of this. Take the most important point first. As far as I am aware, many British NGOs, especially the likes of Christian Aid and Oxfam, have long since accepted the need to address the political and economic or structural roots of poverty. There may at times have been legal constraints on how much they, as charities, could do or say, but they were clear they must do what they could by way of education, research, lobbying and campaigning at home and by supporting organizations in the South prepared to tackle similar tasks on their own home ground. Anti-apartheid, human rights, fair trade, structural adjustment, conflict and disarmament are issues which have long been part of their agendas. They have not been merely 'relief' agencies or 'aid' agencies or 'project-funding' agencies but part of a movement – and often a leading part – for structural change. Maybe it is significant and unfortunate that the most active and practical interface between these NGOs and government has been over aid budgets and funding for relief and fairly small-scale development work. It has probably contributed to a false impression. The argument here, as elsewhere, is surely not 'either/or' but 'both/and'. To respond to the immediate needs of the poor, including the ever-growing number of refugees in the world, is a moral claim on all of us which will never wait till we have put to rights the world's political and economic systems. But to attend only to immediate human needs and not reform the systems which leave those needs unmet and indeed create them is to betray the poor rather than stand by them. It is not even charitable, if charity is acting in the best interests of the neighbours you claim to love. But the argument is not new to the NGOs. They have long rehearsed it themselves.

Two further points should be made in fairness to the NGOs. Granted their efforts to encourage development and deliver basic services like health and education are always bound to be patchy rather than universal, the fact remains that in many situations, if it were left to the governments of developing countries, there would be no such services at all. When governments are said to be the preferred option as partners we should remember that ineffective government is the norm for very poor people. In recent years governments in the South have tried to hand back to development agencies and churches the schools they took over at independence. In recent months one agency reports that the government of Malawi, for example, has closed down a number of hospitals and that the government of Senegal has closed down its state farm input corporation and advisory service. Both have turned to the NGOs to fund these institutions instead; and these are far from isolated examples. So the perfect must not become the enemy of the good. NGOs may well be second-best but they are better than governments which are either incapable or unwilling to serve their people. And all this is even before we come to argue that there are no universal solutions to these problems and that different models and different partnerships may be appropriate in different circumstances. Even the British Labour government on its own home ground finds a mixture of state, private and voluntary provision acceptable when it comes to social services, education and healthcare. Northern NGOs are accused of being something of a mixed blessing to Southern NGOs. They in turn can pin health warnings on direct government funding of Southern NGOs, when it comes to who is likely to foster dependency and inhibit the development of their Southern partners. The NGOs would argue that, if services are delivered in the right way, by working with people and not just for them or over their heads, it can actually build up their skills and organizing abilities. It is a way of 'capability building' and not a way of frustrating it. But if there is a risk, then it is just as real, if not more so, when governments fund Southern NGOs as when Northern NGOs fund them.

There is one further point to make before we leave this discussion about the apparent retreat of the state from the long-established British development agencies, though not from development itself. In one respect over recent years there has been a very significant invasion! For their own good reasons, not least to be able to give good answers to Parliament and the taxpayers when they ask how their money is being spent, governments have demanded more and more of NGOs when agreeing to fund their programmes. They want them managed well; they want their work planned and monitored according to the latest management techniques and logical frameworks; they want thoroughgoing impact studies and evaluations to see what, if anything, has been achieved; they want detailed final reporting; and all of it in the name of accountability. Northern NGOs, if they are to get funding, must do what governments want and in the way governments want it done. She who pays the piper is certainly calling the tune. There are even questions as to whether the government will be willing to fund any of an NGO's work if its campaigning (of which in principle the government very much approves) is likely to go against government policy.

All this may sound reasonable enough but it can subtly at first and then radically alter the ethos of Northern NGOs, and the effects rub off onto Southern NGOs whether funded by Northern agencies or Northern governments. Well-managed programmes, money properly accounted for, and genuine attempts to learn from successes and failures, are important and have not always been given the attention they deserve. But other things are equally worth fighting for, like the thoroughgoing participation of poor communities, which does not always go well with top-down management; like taking risks and trying new ways in very difficult circumstances, which does not always go well with tightly planned programmes; like efforts to empower people and enhance their confidence and self-esteem, which does not always go well with easily aggregated targets; like the unpopular causes and grass-roots voices and awkward questions which governments don't always wish to hear. Northern NGOs may be dismayed at the retreat of the state but they should remain acutely aware of the need to keep the state at arm's length. Of course their mandate is to co-operate wherever possible in the struggle to end poverty but it is not to be merely the arm of the state or its mouthpiece. NGOs are part of civil society, an important countervailing influence to the state, and they should guard their independence. That means amongst other things strengthening their constituencies and drawing as deeply as they can on the support, including the financial support, of the general public. Northern NGOs, like the electorate at large, have a duty to co-operate with government and a duty to disagree with government where necessary. They will only do so adequately from a position of strength which can say 'Let us work together' but can also say 'We have no need of you' and so avoid the very dependency which NGOs are so keen not to foster in others.

The Weakening of the State in the South

So far in my argument I have taken the view that, whilst acknowledging that the state may not be so powerful as it once was, its retreat in the field of development is not the issue; indeed in one area, namely its influence over NGOs in both North and South, its advances may need to be checked. But the focus of this chapter could be equally wrong if we assume that it is the states of the Northern, highly developed countries which are the issue rather than the states of, say, East Asia and, above all, of the developing south, especially of Africa. We need to talk not about the Northern state and overseas development but the Southern state and its own development. In some cases it is difficult to talk about 'retreat' since there is no position to retreat from and states have played little or no constructive role in the recent development of their countries. But if we cannot always talk about 'retreat' we can talk of the 'weakening' and further weakening of the state in at least four respects.

First they have been weakened by the *ideology* that the market rather than the state should be the controlling factor in the economy. This ideology has been fuelled by the collapse of the command economies and the fiscal crisis facing advanced welfare states. This ideology has coloured all their dealings with international financial institutions such as the World Bank and the International Monetary Fund (IMF) which have often forced it upon them. This ideology has allowed transnational corporations, portrayed as the engines of growth, to become political actors with considerable lobbying power and in some cases turnovers larger than those of Third World countries. The result is the inability we noted of Northern governments to act in the face of economic difficulties writ large: 'Business! Do not ask what your government can do for you; ask rather what you can do for your government.'

Second, states in the South have been weakened by *globalization* or what has been called 'the end of geography'. The idea that there are borders over which and within which governments have control has been radically qualified. You can see it happen as poorer countries struggle with the burden of unsustainable debt. It directly affects their capacity for development. If they are to pay back anything at all it will be at the cost of health services and education for their people. The international community is only prepared to cancel or reschedule debts if measures are taken to turn round these failing economies and make them credible members of the global economic order. The conditions are contained in the Structural Adjustment Policies imposed by the World Bank and the IMF. Besides reducing the activities of the state they include opening up their markets to the outside world, lowering protective barriers, and allowing trade and profits to flow more freely, unrestricted by tariffs and border controls. Zones or tax havens are created within which international companies can build factories, hire local labour (though often at low wages and in unsatisfactory conditions) and conduct their business, importing raw materials and exporting products. Countries often compete with each other to attract these companies, lowering import and export duties in the process. The increase in capital flow around the world is another feature of globalization. The free movement of labour is not! When it comes to people moving across borders seeking economic advantages then in many cases the barriers go up. Unimpeded capital flows can be a great advantage to international corporations. They can speculate on the financial markets without seriously investing in a country. They can move their factories rapidly from one country to another, chasing more favourable trading conditions and cheaper labour costs as they go. Such movements tend to disadvantage developing countries in two respects. First these flows are extremely uneven. Most investment in developing countries finds its way to a small minority. Ten developing countries get 75 percent and the whole of Africa gets only 5 percent. Second, capital flight is extremely destabilizing and robs a country of the financial security it needs for steady economic growth and the long-term development of its industries. The Multilateral Agreement on Investment (known as MAI and not now likely to go forward) was designed to address some of these issues. It aimed to secure higher levels of investment for developing countries mainly by ensuring that they created regulations for investors which were clear and consistently upheld so that they knew exactly what they were dealing with and uncertainties were reduced. But any such regulations have also to be attractive. Too many conditions will not help. It is no longer considered sensible, for example, for governments to try to improve the benefits from foreign investment by requiring an investor to buy a minimum proportion of inputs from that country rather than to import them. There must be few sticks and plenty of carrots. The fear is that what allows capital to move in without unnecessary difficulty will by the same token allow it to move out without too many penalties and that there may be more benefits for the offshore speculators than added value for the developing country itself.

The 1997 *World Development Report: The State in a Changing World*,[2] to which we must come in a moment, originally had a chapter on the way in which the power of the state is increasingly constrained by globalization and the growing power of transnational corporations. It was dropped from the final published version but its very existence suggests that at least some World Bank officials recognize that there is legitimate cause for concern. Specific examples include the declining ability of the state to collect taxes. Without such revenues the state cannot supply basic services such healthcare and education. If industry is to be largely free of tax burdens then the only people left to shoulder them are the poor of the land. Or again, if under the rule of privatization the state is expected to see that services are provided but not provide them itself, an inexperienced municipality required to provide water and sanitation is left to deal with the lawyers, financiers and experts of large and highly specialized corporations with all the imbalance of power which that implies. Or again, transnational corporations can inhibit governments from pursuing sensible development and environmental policies. Medical research budgets may be allocated to more expensive and profitable treatments which the wealthy are able and willing to pay for rather than devoted to finding cures for the diseases which do most harm to poorer people. Measures to check global warming may not be taken because of the pressure exerted by coal, oil and nuclear industries which fear they will lose out.

Two other factors besides ideology and globalization have contributed to the weakening of states in the South and their retreat from development. One concerns corrupt and ineffective institutions. They cannot even manage the responsibilities that are left to them; though care should be taken that the state, having been made to give way to market forces, is not now blamed or made a scapegoat for the market's failures. Second, conflict, much of it internal, also weakens the state and can lead to its total collapse as we have seen in countries like Rwanda and Somalia. Both corruption (often seen through highly prejudiced Northern eyes which fail to see the beams and motes in their own) and conflict are easily blamed on irresponsible, perverse and feckless people; but they are closely related to the deep insecurities which ride in on the back of scarce resources; and those scarce resources are in turn closely related to the ever-widening gap between North and South, rich and poor, for which those who cast the stones must bear a good deal of the responsibility.

The State in a Changing World

The subject of the World Bank's World Development Report for 1997 was inspired largely by Japan, one of the chief contributors to World Bank funds. It was concerned that the Bank had given insufficient attention or credit to the role played by the state in what many regarded as the miracle of the tiger economies of South-East Asia (such as China, South Korea, Singapore, Taiwan, Thailand, Malaysia and Indonesia) where the state did not hand over its economic affairs to the market but pursued a state-led model of development, moderating market forces with evident success. The argument has, of course, to be revisited in the light of the present East Asia crisis now reverberating well beyond its borders all round the global economy. Does it prove that the free-market pundits were right and that continuing state intervention was a mistake; or does it only underline the need for the state to control the movement of capital and monitor the extent of external debt in the private as well as the public sector? One outstanding feature of the 1997 World Development Report is that if ideology contributed to the weakening or retreat of the state, as we have been suggesting, then ideology now comes in a rather more nuanced form. Previously the message was simple and straightforward: the state should get out of the way and leave the economy to the markets. Now the message is that an effective state is essential for development. In general it must act as a regulator, consistently applying the known and predictable rules of the game, an enabler, a catalyst and a partner. It should still know its limits (it is no good, for example, at production, marketing and utilities like power, railways and telecommunications) but five fundamental tasks are listed. The state must:

- provide a firm framework of law;
- ensure that the benefits of growth are shared;
- invest in basic services and infrastructure;
- protect the vulnerable;
- protect the environment.

Some will say that this softened ideological stance is more apparent than real. The underlying philosophy of privatization and liberalization remains and the redirection of state activity away from economic management continues as ever before.

Having developed a role for the state, the 1997 report goes on to encourage the state to strengthen its institutions in order to fulfil that role. This is an interesting counterpoint to the earlier emphasis on shrinking and shedding state institutions. Now they are to be strengthened, first by concentrating on essentials and not attempting to do too much (which of course can once again sound like the old argument for privatization in a new guise) and then by carrying them out more effectively. Several measures will encourage better performance including public watchdogs, open competition for jobs in the public sector, better pay to discourage corruption, incentives for public officials to perform better, and a greater responsiveness to the needs of people, including the poorest and marginalized, expressed by way of the ballot box and through increased participation in policy making. Critics of Structural Adjustment Policies have frequently argued that there should be social as well as economic conditions for easing debt and renewing investment in a country. Governments should be required not only to liberalize and regulate the market but to take care of their people. Here in its 1997 report the World Bank seems to take that point in its elaboration of what being an effective state institution involves. These positive suggestions about the role of the state in developing countries have met with an equally positive response from Northern governments including our own. They are now busy funding capacity building programmes which will in time make possible the government-to-government partnerships which they prefer.

Critics of the World Development Report would want a great deal more discussion in at least three areas. *First*, if the state now has a role, it is still a narrow role, largely promoting favourable conditions for the market. Its institutions are still judged almost solely on whether they help or hinder the economy despite comments about being responsive to people and their needs. Development is still limited to economic development. The power of the state is harnessed in the main to corporate interests. Beyond the provision of basic services – and even here the state is warned against overreaching itself – little is said about harnessing the power of the state to the interests of the people: encouraging equality of opportunity and access to information; ensuring adequate food supplies and shelter; guarding their freedom to organize in defence of their rights and working conditions; and protecting minorities.

Second whilst the report recognizes the need to listen to what people have to say and argues for their participation in policy making, the extent of participation seems somewhat limited. It appears to be ruled out altogether when it comes to economic decision making. Neo-liberal policies are self-evidently superior and agreements with the IMF are entrenched and beyond reversal. There is no talking to be done! Participation is not about genuine debate but about persuading people of the benefits of existing policies and winning their consent. Co-operation is to be encouraged in order to improve services and cut costs but the people are largely co-opted into the liberal enterprise. But given the alliance of the state with global market forces and the growing power of international institutions and transnational corporations, people's organizations – or what is often referred to as 'civil society' – need to play a far bigger role than that. Indeed in many parts of the world they are already doing so as people come together to fight for justice, defend democracy and human rights, promote development, respond to human need and claim their right to good governance. The power of the state, however limited, and the power of the private or corporate sector must be balanced by the power of people and, where it is not adequately acknowledged and allowed for in a democratic system, power must be claimed, as it has been from time to time in countries like the Philippines and South Korea, Bangladesh, Nepal and Thailand. Powerful and unaccountable corporate élites cannot have the only say. More popular voices must counter the persistent tendency of the global economy to benefit the rich and the strong rather than the poor and the weak. And to do so effectively, civil society must find ways to organize which are as globalized as the economy. If trade and capital and competition cross borders so must the solidarity and co-operation of people in human development. NGOs, North and South, must now 'internationalize' if they are to be adequate instruments of development in the future.

The *third* area in which the 1997 report is deemed to be deficient concerns global governance. It is generally agreed that markets can be elegant and efficient instruments of economic growth but that they need regulating not just for their own sake but for the sake of the people they are meant to serve. It is also agreed that the nation state has only limited powers as a regulator even when its institutions have been reformed and strengthened. A state within borders cannot regulate a global market which pays less and less attention to borders. Global governance is required for a global market place. Regional, not just national, crises need to be managed. Global stability needs to be promoted. The rights of labour and not just investors need to be ensured. Trans-nationals need to be controlled, not just the arbitrary decisions of state officials which the World Bank fears so much. The environment must be protected – and the cost cannot be borne by the poorer countries. More effective ways must be found of channelling develop-ment assistance. World trade must be reformed and the opportunities in the market place made more equitable. To take one example, the ability of the state to raise taxes to pay for social services and protect the vulnerable and the environment is now very limited as we have seen, especially if much-needed foreign investment is not to be discouraged. This suggests that forms of global taxation should replace local taxation and some by now familiar proposals have been put forward. One is the 'Tobin' tax on the international movement of capital. This could slow it down, encourage responsible longer-term investment which would give industrial develop-ment a chance, and raise revenue to plough back into the developing countries, helping to ensure a more equitable flow of resources to the poor as well as to the rich. Other suggestions include a tax on aircraft fuel or on the use of environmentally sensitive resources such as hardwoods, but they have scarcely got off the ground any more than attempts to minimize the use of exotic financial instruments such as derivatives. The debate, however, must continue. Globalization and its implications for development require not only a report on 'the role of the state in a changing world' but an urgent report on 'global governance' and the strengthening not just of 'state institutions' but of 'global political institutions' with seats at the table for rich and poor alike.

What, then, in summary are we to make of this brief discussion of the 'retreat' of the state in the South rather than in the North in the field of development? First, the state is weak, if not in retreat, and all must play their part, including NGOs, in strengthening its institutions to be reliable and effective within the constraints which globalization has now set. Second, the state should be strengthened to give the market the best possible opportunity to operate in a successful and equitable fashion, but it has a wider role than only that of an economic regulator. Third, a healthy state needs the co-operation but also the countervailing influences of a strong civil society including people's organizations, voluntary societies, churches and NGOs. And fourth, we need to compensate for the very real limits put on the power of the nation state (forcing its 'retreat') by advancing global governance and international co-operation between both governments and civil societies if the global market is to be a social market whose benefits are enjoyed by everyone.

The Retreat of the State from Overseas Development

One Christian's Comments

Since this chapter found its origins within the walls of an English institution which embodies a rather close relationship between the state and Christianity, perhaps this Christian may be allowed a few concluding reflections from the point of view of his Christian faith. There is, of course, no consistent Christian opinion as to whether the state should retreat or advance. Christians can be found among those, like the New Right, who advocate the minimalist state and a return to 'laissez faire' leaving its citizens as far as possible to their own devices; and Christians can be found among the passionate upholders of a highly interventionist state, making itself directly responsible for the welfare of all its citizens as, it is claimed, nothing else can. The Christian Socialist Movement seems to be alive and well and amongst its members are several leading government figures. This variety of opinion is partly due to the fact that Christianity itself is pluralistic. It comes out in many different shapes and sizes. There is no faith but a whole family of faiths and some are more individualistic and others more communitarian in ethos. Again, when Christians have tried to think about the state they have done so in very different circumstances which have certainly influenced their conclusions. The most dramatic example in Christian history was no doubt the division of the Roman Empire leaving a political vacuum in the West which the church duly filled and strong government in the East to which the church became subservient and has remained so in many respects right down to the

present day. Again, Christians come to different conclusions about the state because their faith is not the
only factor to be taken into account. There are social,
political, economic and cultural judgements to be made
so that even when they start from the same convictions
Christians can arrive at quite different conclusions. Yet
another reason why there is no single or settled view is
that Christian judgements like all other judgements are
coloured by vested interests. One view of the state may
appeal to the successful Christian businesswoman and
another to the unemployed churchgoer at her gate; one
state may do for the comparatively wealthy churches of
Northern Europe and another for the impoverished
basic Christian communities of the South. None of us
can escape these influences which inevitably make our
Christian judgements both relative and partial. We can
only strive for integrity between what we say we believe
and how we see the role of the state, and be as open
as possible about both so that others can correct and
complement our views with their own and through argument and dialogue we can achieve together a greater
measure of wisdom. This leads me to make four points.

First, my Christian faith teaches me to expect great
things of human nature but not to trust it too much. It
is made in the image of God and is capable of enormous
generosity, self-sacrifice and creativity. But it is also fatefully insecure and therefore self-centred, using what
power it has, especially collective power, to guard its
own interests, usually at the expense of others. That is
why I remain nervous of too much power in one place
and even more of those who claim the right to exercise

it and to subjugate others be they state or bank or company. That overbearing power is the fundamental root of poverty and injustice which the 'development' movement at its best seeks to overcome. As a result the state can never be allowed to advance too much or remain unchecked any more than market forces driven by the vested interests of powerful companies and entrepreneurs. Power must be carefully checked and balanced if the worst of injustice is to be avoided. That is why in this day and age I am attracted as a Christian to the concept of civil society (without assuming it in turn can go unchecked) as a counterbalance to the state and the market; and I like it better than too much talk of democracy which can be formally practised but nevertheless deny most people any real participation in ordering their life together. It is also why I am attracted to regional and local economies, somewhat internalized, with sufficient muscle of their own to stand up to global market forces.

Second, I am inclined to be fairly pragmatic as a Christian when it comes to deciding how to get things done. Should it be the state, or the private sector, or the voluntary sector or civil society? Should the state provide the services or should they be privatized? Of course the means do not always justify the ends, especially when they ride roughshod over ordinary people; but most decisions about how to get things done involve technical and pragmatic considerations rather than direct deductions from moral or religious principles or any ideology. We should certainly stand on the moral high ground when we debate what we want to achieve: a chance for all human beings to earn a living; to care for their loved ones; to contribute to the common good; to inhabit their own cultures and spiritualities; to fulfil their potential and to know what happiness means. But we should be far less dogmatic about how we achieve it. Whether the state should advance or retreat in development should be judged largely on what I would call 'instrumental' rather than 'ideological' grounds: is it or is it not the best tool for the job? And we should beware of over-generalized answers of the 'never this' or 'never that' variety since they are often signs that an unhelpful 'ideological' judgement is creeping back in.

Third, I do believe there is such a thing as society. I do believe we are members one of another. I do believe that we cannot be human alone and that we are born to relate and to care. That does not automatically make me cast my vote for the advance of the state. It does encourage me to take seriously the question about how best we can act together for the common good. It is a very difficult question to answer in the face of the tendency to care more about my own good than the common good, and in the face of a growing and complex world where the common good is not only the good of my community or nation but the good of the global village or city. But that is the question to ask in relation to the state: not whether it should retreat or advance as such but how we can use it and the powers which are left to it to act together for the good of everyone.

Finally, as a Christian – and not all Christians agree with me – I believe that the key to the future well-being of all humanity is to put the poorest first, or what other Christians, chiefly in the developing countries, have called 'God's priority for the poor'. Put them first, address their poverty before anything else, devise policies which will work for them and all the rest will fall into place. I may have much to say about whether the state should do more or less for instrumental reasons, but in the end I shall judge its fundamental quality according to whether or not the weak and the vulnerable and marginalized are high or low on its agenda. Does it act in ways that run counter to their interests or in their favour? In that sense I have no doubt that the state should advance in the field of development as far and fast and effectively as it possibly can.

Notes

1. Department for International Development, *Eliminating World Poverty: a Challenge for the 21st Century*, White Paper on International Development presented to Parliament by the Secretary of State for International Development ... November 1997, Cm 3789, London, The Stationery Office, 1997.
2. World Bank, *World Development Report 1997: The State in a Changing World*, New York, Oxford U.P. for the World Bank, 1997.

The Retreat of the State in International Affairs

DAVID OWEN

Many nation states in the twentieth century made significant retreats in the exercise of state power in favour of exercising power bilaterally, multilaterally and through specific international organizations. In the main the more powerful the country the more they prefer to exercise power on their own and tend to feel uncomfortable ceding sovereignty within pooled decision-making procedures. This applies in all fields but particularly in security matters and foreign affairs and it is on these areas that I will concentrate.

The United States and International Affairs

In the case of the United States of America the problem in the nineteenth century (and even in the early part of the twentieth century) was first to convert public opinion to the need to exercise power outside their own continent. Secretary of State John Quincy Adams in 1818, before he became President, accurately defined their isolationist tendency, saying:

The Retreat of the State in International Affairs

Wherever the standard of freedom and independence has been or shall be unfurled, there will her [America's] heart, her benedictions and her prayers be. But she goes not abroad, in search of monsters to destroy. She is the well-wisher to the freedom and independence of all. She is the champion and vindicator only of her own.

The generation in Europe that remembers the Vietnam War in the 1960s tends to see a 'gung ho' America and forgets how reluctant the Americans have traditionally been to engage in armed conflict overseas. This reluctance to become involved on the ground in Europe we saw over Bosnia from 1992 to 1995 and again in Kosovo in 1998.

Accepting collective defence commitments is difficult for all countries but particularly the United States. It means undertaking in advance to risk the lives of your countrymen, and to let them die in a foreign field. Military action is the hardest area in which to circumscribe one's national democratic political freedom to manoeuvre but, for smaller countries, combining together offers the only hope, something which Britain found in both world wars against Germany, joining with France and Russia.

We should not forget that, although Canada, Australia and New Zealand sent troops across the oceans in support of Britain's war effort, the United States stayed away for three years. Eventually on 6 April 1917 President Woodrow Wilson signed the Declaration of War which was passed by Congress after a dramatic

Owen

reversal of policy by the President personally saying in his speech to a joint session of Congress: 'The world must be made safe for democracy.' Even so it was not until 2 April 1918, following Lloyd George's appeal to President Wilson, supported by Clemenceau, that the United States' commander, General Pershing, agreed that American troops should be allowed to join the British and French armies in small numbers, prior to having their own army. This army became, in the summer of 1918, the decisive factor in bringing the war to an end that November.

The most significant attempt to dilute national sovereignty in the area of collective defence started after the end of the First World War in the negotiations over the Covenant to establish the League of Nations. In 1919 most people in Europe were ready to accept the leadership of President Woodrow Wilson at the Paris Peace Conference. It was agreed early on in Paris that America's Monroe Doctrine, guaranteeing the United States' supremacy in Latin America, was to remain exempt from the Covenant. The controversy back in the United States came from Article X, the commitment to 'preserve against external aggression the territorial integrity and existing political independence of all members of the League'. This left Wilson wide open to the jibe from Theodore Roosevelt, the former President (who was himself not shy about using America's weight overseas) that 'every time a Yugoslav wishes to slap a Czechoslovak in the face' it would mean that President Wilson would go to war. Wilson thought that the Senate would never dare to reject the whole elaborate structure

100

of the treaties agreed in Paris. But on 19 November 1919 the Senate voted against them. A second vote on 19 March 1920 also failed to pass them. Few events illustrate better the separation of powers in the United States' constitution and the limitations of presidential power as the United States' refusal to join the League of Nations.

American reluctance to be involved once more on the continent of Europe was shown again on 3 September 1939 when Britain's ultimatum to Germany to suspend their attack on Poland expired. While Britain and France declared war President Franklin Roosevelt coincidentally made a proclamation of neutrality similar to that made by President Wilson in 1914. The evacuation from the beaches of Dunkirk in June 1940 and the Royal Air Force's Battle of Britain in August 1940 began to tilt the balance of public opinion in the United States about the war in Europe. But there was still no majority sentiment to become involved. Roosevelt was re-elected on 5 November 1940. In January 1941 he introduced to Congress the Lend-Lease Bill, for financial loans to Britain. After an acrimonious debate, the Bill was eventually pushed through on 11 March 1941. Churchill later described the Lend-Lease Bill in his war memoirs as 'the most unsordid act in the history of any nation'.[1] Its generosity was surpassed only by the post-war Marshall Plan. On 7 December 1941, after 366 Japanese war planes had launched a surprise attack on the United States' Pacific Fleet in Pearl Harbor, Hawaii, America declared war on Japan. It was, however, Germany on 11 December which declared war on the United States which was still neutral in Europe. Churchill's biographer, Martin Gilbert, describes Hitler's decision as 'perhaps the greatest error, and certainly the single most decisive act, of the Second World War',[2] since it brought the United States back to Europe as a belligerent.

With the war over in 1945 the United States started to move their forces back home. They also initially took a rather favourable view of Stalin though disillusionment soon set in. The American people were, however, ready to allow President Harry Truman, with bipartisan support in Congress, to play the key role in the San Francisco Conference in 1945 which established the United Nations. Truman, who had fought in Europe in 1918, carried in his wallet all his life Tennyson's dream, two lines of which are:

Till the war-drum throbb'd no longer and the
  battle-flags were furl'd
In the Parliament of man, the Federation of the
  world.[3]

Winston Churchill called those words the 'most wonderful of prophecies' and his famous 'Iron Curtain' speech in 1946 was devoted to extolling the merits of the United Nations.

In December 1946 the Greek government was losing its civil war in the north against the Greek communists who were operating from mountain strongholds in communist Albania, Bulgaria and Yugoslavia. British aid was drying up and on 21 February 1947 Britain, in deep financial trouble, told the United States that it would have to stop financial aid to Greece and Turkey by the end of March. On 12 March the Truman Doctrine was set out in a speech to a joint session of Congress, establishing one of the primary objectives of American policy as 'the creation of conditions in which we and other nations will be able to work out a way of life free of coercion'. Truman went on to say, 'Should we fail to aid Greece and Turkey in this fateful hour, the effect will be far reaching to the West as well as to the East.' American public opinion now accepted, after losing their own men in two wars fought outside their own territory, that they were not able to insulate their country from world problems. Isolationism gave no protection and, furthermore, even they needed allies to ensure victory. Congressional opinion in 1948 was ready to support the establishment of the North Atlantic Treaty Organization which carried a permanent commitment to the defence of Europe, something they could not accept in 1920. In 1950 North Korea invaded the South and the United States championed a UN response. With the Soviet Union boycotting UN debates under American leadership the UN was the banner chosen under which to fight the Korean War.

Within the international structures that were formed during and since the Second World War the USA always maintained as paramount their intergovernmental nature and in this they have usually been supported by the British, French and Soviets. It was the national veto power which was essential to the United States' support for the UN Charter. Also the consensus decision making without any overriding voting structure was crucial to the American design of the North Atlantic Treaty. This intergovernmental approach was also reflected in the economic structures negotiated at Bretton Woods in 1944, whether in the International Monetary Fund, World Bank or the General Agreement on Tariffs and Trade. It was automatic that the United States would provide the Supreme Allied Commander in Europe (SACEUR) for NATO, given that Winston Churchill in 1943 had felt it essential that an American general was in overall charge for D-Day and the push towards Berlin until the unconditional surrender of the German forces. It is a United States' Congressional demand that all American military combat personnel remain ultimately under American commanders and the President.

Nation States

International political comment discussing the phenomenon of globalization sometimes naively claims that we have reached or will soon reach the natural end of the nation state. Yet time after time events show such predictions false. The world's only superpower, the United States of America, far from questioning the nation state, has enlarged its structure and retained its identity, shape and cohesion throughout a century when it has accepted, albeit reluctantly, an increasing world role. On the continent of Europe the Treaty of Rome has the most supranational features in the world. Yet most of the politicians of the fifteen members of the European Union claim in public to wish to retain the nation state, albeit with reduced powers. In trade negotiations the European Commission negotiates for all countries in the EU and in the European Single Market qualified majority voting, accepted even by Margaret Thatcher, predominates. Even the Benelux countries, while often talking the language of supranationalism, nevertheless have national interests which they vigorously defend. Norway has twice in a national referendum rejected its government's advice to join the EU. In Denmark successive governments have found it harder and harder to ratify treaties which undercut the powers of the Danish Parliament. Sweden is starting to experience the same suspicion of supranationalism, and not just on membership of a single currency which they initially signed up to at Maastricht.

New states around the world are also emerging all the time. The collapse of the Berlin Wall saw the reunification of Germany and, despite the continuing economic difficulties of the Eastern part, we are seeing a new self-confident but unthreatening assertion of Germany's legitimate rights and powers as a nation state. The break-up of the former Yugoslavia has brought about five new nations: Slovenia and Croatia are ethnically homogeneous; the other three, Yugoslavia, Macedonia and Bosnia-Herzegovina, are still ethnically divided. The demise of the Soviet Union saw fifteen new nations emerge and the re-establishment of a Russian national identity. Czechoslovakia split into two with a so-called 'velvet divorce'. Membership of the UN, which at its foundation in 1945 stood at fifty-one states, has seen a steady expansion in its size and now in 1998 has 185 states.

Yet despite these clear manifestations of nationhood we still hear from those who seek to denigrate and diminish the nation state. The critics often choose as their focal point the unattractive aspects of nationalism, whether it be fascism, racism, xenophobia or chauvinism. They conveniently forget that fascism was defeated by the readiness of people to die in defence of their nation – in the United Kingdom after the fall of France, in Russia after the Germans came to the outskirts of Moscow and fatefully after Pearl Harbor when the United States' forces were attacked in the Pacific. British lives were also lost in post-war fighting in Korea, in the confrontation in Malaysia, in recapturing the Falkland Islands and in the service of the United Nations.

A nation, whether democratic or not, has as one of its most distinctive features a readiness to fight to defend its territory when under attack. The most profound decision in a democracy is that which politicians take to send their nation's children (often including their own) off to war. That is one reason why democracies are said to be slow to fight. After the wanton sacrifice of the First World War, Wilfred Owen and other poets have made us establish a new language for war. Today very few would claim: '*dulce et decorum est pro patria mori.*' Nonetheless, when the threat is real, a duty of collective self-responsibility asserts itself. A mutual identity, a sense of collective self-regard and self-responsibility is the hallmark of a nation. A multi-national state can best build those characteristics within a democratic framework, but it is harder to achieve and sometimes founders where there are internal ethnic divisions. The character and unity of a nation depend a great deal on how it retains its identity. No wise political leader will dare take the collective will to fight for granted or lightly invoke it. The best protection against the irresponsible sacrifice of the nation's young in a democracy is that the wrath of the family will be visited through the ballot box on politicians who act irresponsibly.

In any analysis of what can be sound and sensible retreats in the power of the state in international affairs, one needs to be sure that nothing is done which damages the basic instinct for self-preservation, nor erodes the collective will to fight in one's own national self-defence. Also one needs to consider whether a retreat in the power of the state deepens, or weakens, the democratic way of life of the nation; democracy of itself makes a massive contribution to the collective will to defend what one respects and identifies with. Democracy is the system whereby individuals can best relate to the national interest, for it is far easier to act unselfishly and accept constrains if there is a system of governance premised on strict accountability to freely agreed majority opinion.

A United States of Europe?

The European Union in its development so far represents a unique attempt to marry the strengths of individual nationhood with the merits of nations combining together. The founding fathers and some of the politicians at the time of the Messina Conference, which established the Treaty of Rome, did envisage that the commitment to an ever greater unity would inexorably lead to a nation called 'Europe' developing in the fullness of time, but they avoided spelling that out in treaty form. A pragmatic step by step approach to the evolution of the future has governed all subsequent treaties. As a direct consequence of this there is a calculated ambivalence as to whether we are creating a union of European nation states or a 'United States of Europe'. It is as legitimate to argue that the EU's destiny is to remain a union with limits to the retreat from nationhood, as it is to argue that the EU's destiny is to continue the retreat until it is a United States of Europe. It is a travesty to say, however, that those who argue for limits are Euro-sceptics. I am not a Euro-sceptic but rather an enthusiastic supporter of building a consensus on as many issues as possible with our nearest neighbours in Europe; I defy anyone to challenge my political record as a convinced champion of the EU. But I am just as proud to fight within the EU to retain the sinews of British nationhood and to set limits on the retreat of our state. I look to the politicians in the House of Commons today, in 1998, to retain the self-confidence to use the veto powers contained within the treaties and to block moves that erode the essentials of our national identity. One of the main reasons that I supported the Maastricht Treaty is that it sets limits to the retreat of the nation state.

The Retreat of the State in International Affairs

The Participation of the UK

In 1956 we in the United Kingdom chose, with few dissenters, not to participate in the creation of what was initially the Common Market. Geography dictated we stay outside the Coal and Steel Community which did so much to bring the great industries of France and Germany together across their national boundaries. History stopped us from being active at the Messina Conference. In 1962 the UK did, however, embark on a genuine debate about whether we should join the Common Market and the two politicians of their time who, by nature, dissembled least faced up to the unresolved issue of federalism with honesty. Hugh Gaitskell, then Leader of the Labour Party, replying to Prime Minister Harold Macmillan's television broadcast, said that, if Macmillan wanted to enter a European federation, it would mean the 'end of Britain as an independent nation' and that we would become 'no more than "Texas" or "California" in the United States of Europe'. Jo Grimond, then Leader of the Liberal Party, put the contrary view: that if we were going to 'control the running of Europe democratically', we would have to 'move towards some form of federalism', adding 'If anyone says different to that they are misleading the public.' Would that many of the politicians who came after had had the same honesty. In what I once called the politics of 'fudge and mudge' it has become an art form in the UK to obfuscate. Too many politicians deny the pressures within the Brussels bureaucracy to undermine the nation state. Before the signatures on the Maastricht Treaty were dry

David Owen

many Continental politicians were trying to erode the three intergovernmental pillars which they had only reluctantly accepted. To say this is not to be paranoid or to believe in conspiracy theories. To their credit on the Continent most politicians are quite open about their federalist intentions. On the single currency, the British and Danish opt-out in the Maastricht Treaty reflected in the main a number of differences of view. Firstly, whether it was possible to run a single currency success-fully across eleven national boundaries without inevi-tably moving towards single economic and fiscal policies. Also there was a concern that these economic and fiscal decisions would not be made democratically without a federalist structure. In addition there were important technical economic questions. Adoption of a single currency across national boundaries involves a fundamental political change of direction for the UK and it is right that this should be made outside the con-fines of party politics and requires a referendum. The onus of proof has been placed on those who want to give up the pound to show real benefits if such a refer-endum is ever called. The implications of a single currency for the security and foreign policy intergovern-mental pillars is something on which I will concentrate in this chapter, leaving the economic and fiscal questions to one side.

Implications of a Single Currency

I am certain that majority voting designed to produce a single, as distinct from a common, foreign and security policy is an absolute Rubicon for a nation state. Cross it and you have given up your nationhood even though some politicians will not admit this. As to a single currency, my deep suspicion is that, though in my judgement it is not a Rubicon, for those countries who take it, it will prove to be a threshold decision, a decision on a slippery slope where unless the foreign and security intergovernmental pillar is reinforced the slide will be towards a United States of Europe. The nature of the economic and fiscal decisions necessary for convergence will drive those who choose to live in 'Euroland' to develop most of the characteristics of a nation called 'Europe' and in that process they will be even more relaxed than they are at present about introduced qualified majority voting in the framework of a common foreign and security policy.

Some people argue that there is no danger of the foreign and security intergovernmental pillar eroding in Euroland, but it is not hard to see how this erosion would happen. In the Maastricht Treaty there is a potentially far-reaching provision for declaring an area of foreign policy to be the subject of joint action. This decision has, however, to be taken unanimously but thereafter the implementing decisions are to be taken by qualified majority voting. The mechanism was wished on the UK at Maastricht by those who saw this mechanism as the thin end of a potentially very long wedge. The temptation to invoke joint action will come at a time when the UK has a very strong foreign policy objective and wants the EU to support it. It is not hard to imagine others in the EU suggesting that this policy should only be adopted if it is to be subject to joint action. It only then requires a Foreign Secretary who either believes in Euroland, or is too ready to accept the advice of a Foreign Office often eager to go along with the European consensus and manifesting a difficulty with ever exercising a veto, and the UK will have crossed the all important threshold, that is qualified majority voting in foreign policy. I have no doubt that the UK should never under any circumstances, however tempting, cross that threshold, but I cannot be sure, given the past history of us being edged over similar thresholds, that we will not do so. There is a strong argument for the UK Parliament restricting the right of any government in this area and insisting that joint action can never be declared without the prior approval of both Houses of Parliament. Such a government constitutional commitment could do something to retain confidence prior to any government deciding that they wish to call a referendum on the single currency. But even with that constitutional safeguard would a Britain operating within a single currency feel as free to conduct its own foreign policy? Would it be prepared to support the United States when the rest of Europe did not support American policy? In concrete terms would Britain have been able to adopt the same military and sanctions policy from the moment Iraq invaded Kuwait in 1990 and for the rest of the decade? I very much doubt if it would have done so. Most of Europe did not contribute to the force that threw out the Iraqis and even French participation was in doubt for some considerable time. Over Kosovo we have seen a similar reluctance to commit troops and to be ready to use them in support of diplomatic ends.

Each EU nation needs to have an inner self-confidence to step out of an otherwise EU consensus position on foreign and defence policy. There can be no doubt that a country whose currency is part of the Euro will be under additional pressures to avoid the tough choices of following an independent foreign policy line that carries risks of trade embargoes of economic discrimination. This is the case for one simple reason: retaliation on a participating member in the single currency will no longer affect only that country but *all* participants. It can be argued, therefore, and sometimes is, that countries operating within a monetary union have more economic protection to take a robust foreign policy line, but EU experience shows that what is more likely to develop is a soft common foreign and security policy designed to keep national policy within the middle of the Euro pack, something which we have seen all too recently over Kosovo. One does not need to invoke British foreign policy over the last one thousand years. Instead, one only has to recall (with the exception of France) the continental European equivocation over nuclear weapons while we were still confronting the Soviet Union in the 1970s and 1980s to know why we should refuse to lose our independence in foreign and defence policy. While the French also know this to be true and are sympathetic to British fears, in the last analysis they believe that Germany will always support France out of solidarity if French vital interests are at stake; Britain has no such bilateral buttress. Some in Britain dream of joining the Franco-German alliance. It is now said that because of the SPD (Social Democratic Party) victory in Germany we will be able to develop a trilateral relationship with France and Germany to match the bilateral Franco–German relationship; but Oscar Lafontaine comes from the Saarland and is very close to France in all respects. Gerhard Schröder is more sympathetic but will find the German bureaucracy totally set on the primacy of the Franco-German alliance. Whitehall is now beginning to adjust its language and talk of a quadrilateral relationship including Italy, but this will cause even more resentment across the European Union.

The wise decision of Tony Blair, as Prime Minister, to put the onus in a referendum on demonstrating concrete benefits means that the proponents, instead of talking about 'missing the train', or failing to 'catch the bus' or building up a vague belief that joining the Euro is inevitable, will have to answer hard questions of national interest. Also the new proposals from the Neill Committee on Standards in Public Life mean that there will be rules in place on the fair conduct of any referendum. Personally I eschew fixing any timetables; I hope Britain never has to be part of a single currency and, only if the economic disadvantages that I foresee prove to be unjustified and the political ramifications are less than I fear, would I be prepared to contemplate it.

Prudence would dictate first seeing how countries, whose economies are not converging with the majority within the Euro, weather an economic downturn, without the capacity to devalue their currency or to alter their interest rates. Similarly how will such countries ease rising unemployment without migration possibilities to other EU countries that are available, for example, to workers in the United States' East Coast rust belt, where they are able to move down South or out West? Also how might one judge the effect on unemployment of not having the fiscal transfers between the countries of Europe that exist between the prosperous and rich states in the United States? Waiting and seeing means judging that it is not sufficient to accept the arguments of these for those politicians who want to join and who mouth bland generalities about political will and the need not to be left behind in Europe. Not joining the Euro is in no way comparable to staying away from the Messina Conference which set up the Common Market in 1956. Today in 1998 we are full members of the EU and we have helped to shape the European Monetary Union for those countries who want to join. We are entitled to join the single currency if we wish at any time after fulfilling the criteria within the Maastricht Treaty. There cannot be any veto from another EU country on our joining. In the same way that over the Exchange-Rate Mechanism (ERM) we participated in the European Monetary System (EMS) and kept our options open to join as and when we wished, so we do not need to use a veto: all we need is self-confidence and the will to exploit the Euro to our commercial benefit as we have done the dollar and the yen.

We do need to watch carefully how other countries behave on all aspects of the EU's political development. In that sense we will be better able to assess the political impact of monetary union and the certainty of our being able to continue to pursue an independent foreign policy after the passage of the years. Our political leaders need the confidence to wait and see and not be carried away by an illusion that leadership is always about action. Some of the best leaders are those who understand the power of patience. Claims to leadership in Europe usually turn out to be transient or illusory. We lead best on the many issues where the United States' policy is a major factor not because we have an exclusive relationship with the USA but because of a national affinity on most, but not every, issue.

We must also not feel too threatened by loose talk that our place in the G7 will be put in jeopardy if we are not part of the single currency. Canada will not easily give up G7 participation. Nor would I be that confident that Germany, France and Italy, when the single currency is operating, will agree to be represented by the President of the European Bank or one Prime Minister; unless, of course, they appoint or elect, as many wish, a Euroland Cabinet with a President and Finance Minister. Russia has only just secured its G8 position and its power will slowly recover. If an informal G3 of the dollar, yen and Euro develops, so be it. We have lived in the UK with the reality for some years where the Deutchsmark has given the German Bundesbank and German government a stronger role on international monetary matters than the UK. Nevertheless, an independent Governor of the Bank of England operating a successful economy with a strong pound will find a welcome in most monetary forums and a British Prime Minister's political influence in G8 will continue to have real value.

Britain does not have to stay in a bunker while exercising its Euro opt-out. Instead it should champion and develop further the common, not single, foreign and security intergovernmental pillar. We can demonstrate that in this area Britain is not a negative but a positive reformer, ready to become a key player within the EU. We should talk intensively with the French and I suspect we can both learn from the dialogue over what was called the 'Fouchet Plan' even though it was held in 1962. The Fouchet Plan failed because of a dispute over limiting the supranationality of a 'union of states'. Now such a debate will in some matters be easier, since the parameters of the EU are much better defined. France wants Britain to be more forthcoming over European defence; Britain's defence partnership on the ground with France from 1992 onwards in Bosnia, as I witnessed at close quarters, has left both armed forces with considerable mutual respect. The far closer working relationship between the Foreign and Commonwealth Office and the Quai d'Orsay established in 1991 with the break-up of Yugoslavia has meant that the old scars from the failed collaboration over Suez in 1956 have largely healed. Paris has noted with both surprise and appreciation the readiness of London to differ seriously at times with the Washington line over Yugoslavia. It is essential for Britain that we build on this relationship with France, which should not in any way be based on downplaying the USA or diminishing Germany, let alone being antagonistic to NATO. It is in our interest to ensure that the intergovernmental pillar supporting a common foreign and security policy is bedded into the

David Owen

practice and future development of the EU. A wise British government would quietly let our European friends know that this needs to be done before the UK will ever seriously contemplate participating in a single currency.

The Western European Union

So, the logic for holding a defence organization like the Western European Union (WEU) in reserve for action in support of EU diplomacy, if the United States do not want to use NATO, is compelling. The EU–WEU defence organization should not attempt to replace NATO or the UN. In 1996/97 carefully crafted steps were taken whereby the WEU would in future be enabled to use NATO assets and infrastructure for various peacekeeping and peacemaking tasks without American participation. This bottom-up approach is working; it is important that it continues to do so, for given the quality of NATO's assets, which are in all important respects American, it is hard to see any serious European defence operation being successful without these assets. If Britain works with those EU partners, like France, who attach importance to the subordination of the WEU to the intergovernmental foreign, defence and security pillar of the EU, they will find that the French want to see the WEU role going beyond peace-keeping; Britain should accept this. The 1948 Treaty of Brussels which established the WEU, and which could become part of the EU treaties, has a firmer defence commitment binding its members to go to the defence of any of their number who is attacked than is contained even in the 1949 treaty that established NATO. An advantage of retaining the treaty in its present form is that signatory countries may not have to submit an adaptation to the EU for ratification through a refer-endum. The French will want a mechanism whereby both their nuclear deterrent and that of the British are put at the service of the EU. This is a long-overdue reform and an important guarantee now that Russian nuclear forces are less powerful and now that the American nuclear guarantee for Europe is, therefore, arguably less likely to be invoked. Some countries, including Sweden, Finland and Ireland, may well want to opt out of any defence arrangement within the EU; this should be accepted without demur although opinion in those countries on this issue is changing. The essential pre-requisite is to retain the WEU's own democratic assembly made up of parliamentarians from national parliaments. Britain must insist that this type of assembly be taken into any EU structure so as to main-tain the existing forums for democratic parliamentary accountability for EU defence matters. It would also buttress the maintenance of an effective intergovern-mental common foreign and security policy in the pro-cess. It will also make national parliamentarians more receptive to the European Parliament having primacy on Single Market issues and ensure national parliaments have some involvement with the intergovernmental common foreign and security policy pillar. Many members of the European Parliament and the European Commission will oppose such a step. In doing so they

David Owen

will be downplaying the advantage of having national parliaments tied in to an important aspect of European activity. Within the EU few things worth having ever come about without horse-trading and in essence that is the basis of the art of most politics. The UK government must, therefore, engage constructively with our partners on defence but insist on retaining the essentials of governmental decision making and not allow the European Commission, the European Parliament or the European Court have any locus on defence within the EU treaties.

It will be the generation of people untouched by the Cold War who will decide the limits to the UK's future role within the European Union and the extent of any further retreats. We who lived through the most testing period of deterrence and détente, by confronting the Soviet Union, have a duty as far as possible to ensure that the younger generation make their decision in the full possession of all the facts, against the background of a UK that has rebuilt a strong economic base and has redeveloped a broad, confident, global outlook.

Notes

1. *The Second World War, vol 2 Their Finest Hour*, by Winston S. Churchill, Cassell, 1949, p 503.
2. *Second World War*, by Martin Gilbert, Weidenfeld and Nicolson, 1989, p. 277.
3. 'Locksley Hall' in Tennyson, *The Complete Poetical Works of Tennyson*, London, Oxford U.P., 1953 reprinted with the title *Poems and Plays* 1965, p 94.

Theological Afterword

STEPHEN PLATTEN

The English often appear to exhibit paradoxical feelings about their own sense of nationality and the role of the state. 'An air of superiority combined with a disingenuous tendency toward understatement' is the criticism often offered, and particularly from the other side of the Atlantic. Indeed, until the recent outbreak of 'devolution fever' in the late 1990s, the English were almost entirely unselfconscious about their nationhood. It is only talk of Scottish independence and of self-government for the Welsh that has made some in England begin to reflect upon how 'Englishness' and 'Britishness' might be distinct. For much of the world nationhood is a relatively modern experience; even in Europe both Germany and Italy have existed as nation states for less than one hundred and fifty years. Despite this relatively short experience of nationhood in many countries, the nineteenth and twentieth centuries have seen more than their share of traumas in bringing nation states to birth. What degree of centralized planning and government is appropriate and how autonomous should nations be in settling their own affairs? The transformation of Europe in 1989 and the tragic conflicts in the

Balkan states which have followed further indicate how difficult it is to answer such questions.

The Church and the Role of the State

Over two millennia, the Christian Church has engaged variously with the issue of the state; references both in the Gospels and in the writings of Paul[1] give early evidence of this. In the Western Church one of the foundation documents was St Augustine of Hippo's *City of God*,[2] written in the early fifth century, following the fall of Rome to Alaric. Augustine's earthly and heavenly cities are distinct and, in differing degrees since, the Western Church has held itself at arm's length from the organs of the state. In the East, the Byzantine model has been one of close co-operation or even collusion; it was such a model that continued in Russia, Romania, Bulgaria and elsewhere during the Soviet era, often giving the churches a tarnished reputation through accusation of collaboration with totalitarian régimes. The issues of the role and power of the modern state has been responded to by Christian leaders and thinkers in a variety of ways as Michael Taylor hints towards the end of his chapter. In the work of Professor Bryan Griffiths here in Britain and of Michael Novak in the USA the insights of the New Right are fully embraced within a broad Christian framework – Anglican in the case of Griffiths and Roman Catholic for Novak. Others, including some 'liberation theologians', have allowed Marxist analysis to colour their thought. In the light of these contrasting responses, what might one make of the debate outlined in these chapters in the context of Christian theology and moral thought?

Perhaps the first key point to register is that the churches have themselves been integral to the whole process of the 'advance of the state'. The process now generally styled 'secularization' has empirically seen the state assuming responsibility for a number of areas of life where the church had been a pioneer. In relation to these chapters this is most obvious in the areas of health, education and welfare. Some would argue cynically that the churches took initiatives in these realms since they represented the interests of the ruling classes; the upper middle classes feared civil unrest and so the development of education and the provision of reasonable welfare was advocated as a form of social control. Doubtless there is truth in this claim but as a general theory it is historically reductionist, and a broader survey would suggest that, over the centuries and beginning with the work of the monasteries, Christianity has believed there to be imperatives in these areas; these imperatives are implied within the framework of Christian teaching. It is interesting to note that before the growth of the modern nation state those same monastic resources helped in the development of industry and farming (and thus economic growth); the Cistercians in particular showed a remarkable degree of organization and initiative which would lay the foundations for the growth of industry in early modern Europe.

From the nineteenth century onwards, then, the state began to assume responsibility in these areas. The advent of the 1870 Forster Education Act was a milestone in the state's assumption of responsibility in this area of life; even then, however, the system established remained a dual system and this was enshrined in statute law with the 1902 Education Act when some nonconformists complained that this was the first step toward 'Rome on the rates'! This development in education was part of a broader process of secularization; this process describes the advance of the state, the movement towards 'big government', from which it is now argued by many that the modern nation state should withdraw. The churches have continued to pioneer in some initiatives relating to welfare and health – terminal care is a classic example – but generally the twentieth century has seen a retreat of Christianity from this area of human endeavour. This has left the churches freer to offer a critique of the socio-political status quo from the point of view of the Christian gospel. When the churches have done this most effectively they have taken into account the empirical evidence and indeed the shifts in economic and political culture. Theological reflection that has ignored economics and other empirical factors has always been unconvincing in its resulting critique.

Christian Attitudes to the Role of the State

Historical Background

Earlier on, we hinted at differing attitudes amongst Christian theologians in this area of the role of the state and economic planning. The Reformation had a radical impact upon such attitudes. Martin Luther established a pattern of thought focused in his doctrine of the 'two kingdoms' within which the church and the secular state were seen to be two quite distinct realms within which the providence of God operated differently. It is argued that this theory was one of the factors which contributed to the quietism and the collusion of the German churches with Hitler's régime during the Nazi period. In contrast to this, Calvin's reformed theology issued, in theocratic government in sixteenth-century Geneva, a pattern which would be unthinkable in contemporary pluralist societies. Sociologist Max Weber drew out from Calvinism his sociological and economic theory enshrined in the so-called 'Protestant Work Ethic' and set out in his *The Protestant Ethic and the Spirit of Capitalism*;[3] the success of capitalist economics was rooted by Weber in the values promulgated by Calvinist reformed theology and the polity engendered by it.

The Common Good, Subsidiarity, Solidarity

If the above theories are seen to be different means of describing and commenting upon the phenomena encountered in contemporary western society, then the churches have also evolved different critiques of these same phenomena. The keynote document from the Roman Catholic tradition[4] was Pope Leo XIII's encyclical *Rerum Novarum* (1891). Rooted in the natural law theory adumbrated by St Thomas Aquinas, this encyclical developed the notion of the 'common good'. Natural law assumes that certain patterns of moral behaviour lead to the flourishing and fulfilment of individuals; the common good builds upon this within the context of the wider community. We contribute to the common good because we want to live in a society which is fair and just. As such, the service of the common good is an end in itself. The merits of natural law and the common good are that they are rooted in arguments based upon practical reason and thus open to people of all traditions and not just those within the Christian churches.

So significant was Leo XIII's encyclical for social thought in the Roman Catholic Church that many of the documents which have enshrined Roman Catholic social teaching in the twentieth century have been dated from that seminal statement on Catholic social teaching. So Pius XI's encyclical of 1931 was titled *Quadragesimo Anno*. It was this document which first coined the use of the term 'subsidiarity', now so popular within the thinking of the European Commission. Subsidiarity asserts that decisions should be taken at the lowest level possible which is compatible with good government. Such a theory would support avoidance of big government and encourage the regionalization developed by Vincent Watts in the introduction. Later encyclicals, and notably those from the pontificates of John XXIII, Paul VI and John Paul II have all developed this pattern of social teaching. The common good, subsidiarity and, more recently, 'solidarity' have remained key concepts. As time has passed, so biblical theology has increased its influence within Roman Catholic social teaching, further affirming the common good.[5] Pope Paul VI's brilliant encyclical *Evangelii Nuntiandi* embraced some of the principles enunciated by liberation theologians in the 1960s and 1970s. Issues raised in the chapter by Michael

Taylor begin to be encompassed within this strand of
Catholic social thought, moving the limits of such teaching out beyond the narrow boundaries and interests of
individual nation states into the realm of international
economic development.

Concern for the Underprivileged

Emerging over a similar time span was a rather different
but complementary tradition within Anglican and
Reformed theology. This often began with an acknowl-
edgement of the 'fall' of humanity and thus the need to
protect the weakest within society from the selfishness
of human nature. Within Anglicanism this was pion-
eered by members of the Christian Socialist Movement.
In some ways this tradition was neither *socialist* nor a
movement as we might normally understand these
terms. Instead it was a succession of thinkers and acti-
vists – F. D. Maurice, Henry Scott Holland, Stewart
Headlam, St John Groser, R. H. Tawney and others –
who believed that Christian belief has implications for
the ordering of society and not only for the personal
morals of individuals; within this compass there is generally a particular concern for the poor and the underprivi-
leged. One could argue that this tradition reached
maturity in the writings of R. H. Tawney and most
notably in his *Religion and the Rise of Capitalism*.[6]
Tawney's thought began from Christian doctrinal beliefs
and notably in the affirmation that human beings are
made in the image of God. Tawney saw this, however,
within the social context of human endeavour and

placed human aspirations against the background of the fallenness of human nature. Despite some naiveté in Tawney's thought, characterized by him being captured by an overhistorical view of the Church, still his writings influenced the emerging concept of the 'welfare stare'. In the period before the publication of the Beveridge Report, Tawney, William Temple, J. H. Oldham and others were key influences in the social thought which issued in the emergent welfare state in the work of the post-war Labour government. It is this trend about which Arthur Seldon has clear reservations in his chapter.

Christian Realism

This stream of thought, which might be characterized by the phrase 'Christian realism', has, however, been a far more marked feature of the North American scene in the twentieth century. The thought of Reinhold Niebuhr, his associates and disciples, begins, once again, from a realistic account of the fallenness of humanity. It is set out in Niebuhr's classic analysis of 1932, *Moral Man and Immoral Society*.[7] Niebuhr is clear that the Christian gospel can offer hope and aspiration for humanity and that this stands at the heart of the offering of Christ himself. All this, however, is set against the background of human fallibility and the need to be realistic in responding to this. The human will-to-power requires the use of coercion by the state if order and justice are to prevail. Despite his liberal pragmatic economic analysis, Nigel Lawson is keen to assert the need for the effective rule of law and for the support of property rights within a democratic society. Parallel to this, Niebuhr summarizes his moral and political instincts in a well-known quotation: 'Man's capacity for justice makes democracy possible; but man's inclination to injustice makes democracy necessary.' Niebuhr was unashamed in allowing Christian theological reflection to impinge upon political issues. Indeed, his theological thought was as much formed through his ministry in the great motor car factories in Detroit as it was by the broader stream of the Christian moral and theological tradition. This has led some to criticize Niebuhr for allowing the cultural patterns of liberal western democracy to compromise the historic truths of Christian teaching. Nonetheless, it is the case that Christian belief has always and necessarily developed within, and adapted itself to, the context of the culture in which it has lived.

This is manifestly the case with the thought of Reinhold Niebuhr, and it is also almost certainly the reason why his thought influenced politicians as widely different from each other as John F. Kennedy, R. A. Butler and Tony Benn, as well as numerous writers in social ethics. Niebuhr always balanced realism with idealism and his thought is well crystallized in the prayer for which he also became well known:

> God, give me the serenity to accept the things I cannot change, the courage to change the things I can, and the wisdom to know the difference.

The application of Niebuhr's particular brand of
Christian realism can add a cogent critique within this
wider debate about the retreat of the state. His acknowl-
edgement of the importance of coercion suggests the
need for intervention, so that the economic effects of
the market are mitigated at certain points under the
influence of wider moral considerations. At the heart of
the New Testament is the moral imperative flowing from
an emphasis on *self-giving love*; the ultimate issue of
this lies in the passion and crucifixion of Jesus. This
requires an emphasis on compassion which economics
alone cannot offer. Niebuhr's pragmatism also allows
for empirical considerations such as those outlined by
Nigel Lawson, Arthur Seldon (and, in a different way,
Michael Taylor) to be taken into consideration. Furthermore, Niebuhr was no pacifist and echoed much of what
David Owen argues on isolation and intervention in
international relations.

The 'Soul of Europe'

These brief reflections may indicate why the Christian
theologian might wish to contribute to this debate about
the role of the state in each of the areas addressed in
the earlier chapters. These reflections also suggest that
the theological and moral critique so developed has
implications for each of the issues involved. Jacques
Delors, when he was President of the European Commission, often spoke of the need to work also for the
'soul of Europe'. Although he himself is a practising
Roman Catholic, his vision was never narrow nor exclu-

sive. In referring to the 'soul of Europe' he referred to the deep religious impulses within humanity which allow human beings to reflect upon society at a level beyond that of the purely pragmatic and empirical. The Christian gospel has something essential to contribute to the current debate. Roman Catholic social teaching with its emphasis on the common good, on solidarity and subsidiarity may be combined with the Christian realist tradition to argue that economic theory alone is insufficient as a means of setting the scene for just and equitable patterns within contemporary society. The contribution of economic theory is crucial and it may be that inappropriate intervention and manipulation of the market has hampered effective growth. Nevertheless, other issues must also impinge; these include essential contributions of compassion and generosity at the heart of the Christian message, and a clear option for the poor. We shall, therefore, focus in our conclusion on three issues influenced by this imperative, which appear to remain intractable as we enter the third millennium. These issues are those of war and peace, world poverty and justice.

Is *the State in Retreat?*

As this book is being put together for publication, the Balkan tragedy continues to unfold with the bombing of Serbia, the ethnic cleansing of Kosovo and vast oceans of refugees pouring into Western Europe. David Owen's reflections make salutary reading. America has abandoned her isolation but the uncertainty over the use of

land forces and the paucity of overall strategy suggest
that the fears that fuelled isolation remain there in the
background. Issues about the autonomy of nation states
have been reopened by NATO's decision to intervene
in what it believes to be a radical injustice, albeit within
a sovereign state. Christian leaders and theologians have
posed sharp questions about the nature of this conflict
as a 'just war'. Neither the conditions of it being waged
by a lawful authority nor its proportionate aims are
clear; the United Nations was not consulted for its support and the lack of clarity in the strategy raises questions about proportion. There is not the space here to
develop these arguments in detail, nor indeed is there
yet sufficient clarity about the facts. The question of a
government or governments intervening in international
affairs, indeed even in the affairs of a sovereign state,
however, remains stark. Certainly this hardly looks like
retreat.

Questions relating to the world's poorest nations are
brought into focus by the remarkable stamina mani-
fested by those who lead the 'Jubilee' campaign for the
forgiveness of Third World debt. The issues raised by
Michael Taylor continue to be pursued, and commen-
tators in both the realms of economics and theology
begin to believe that some movement is possible.
Germany has ceased to block movements to forgive
debt. On the local level, similar issues of poverty are
raised by Arthur Seldon. If nations have overenthusiast-
ically embraced welfare, removing incentives for individuals and developing a 'nanny state', how shall we
safeguard the well-being of the poor and most vulner-

able in the developed world if welfare systems are to be dismantled, or, in developing countries, how will starvation and extreme poverty be mitigated without the building of some form of welfare infrastructure?

Finally, Nigel Lawson refers obliquely to what is generally called 'commutative justice'; property rights should be protected and so should the rule of law. Poverty and international conflict, however, also raise issues of distributive justice. The figures for the North and South in our contemporary world have frequently been published and Michael Taylor alludes to these. In all of these matters the Christian theologian is not there to subvert or to replace the role of the economist and political theorist, rather like a latter-day creationist implying that the Genesis narrative is a scientific theory in competition with Darwin. Instead the Christian theologian should (on the basis of a full understanding of the empirical information in these areas) offer a constructive critique that contributes to thinking on the role of the state in a manner which is neither ideological nor romantic. Christian moral reflection should offer constructive proposals which might contribute towards a compassionate 'soul for the world'.

Notes

1. Matthew 22:21; Mark 12:17; 20:25; Romans 13:1–7.
2. St Augustine of Hippo, *The City of God*, trans. Henry Bettenson, Harmondsworth, Penguin Books, 1972.
3. Max Weber, *The Protestant Ethic and the Spirit of Capitalism*, London, Allen and Unwin, 1930.

4. For a good account of Roman Catholic social ethics since 1891 see *The New Politics*, ed Paul Vallely, London, SCM Press, 1998.
5. The passage in Acts 4:32–5 is often quoted.
6. R. H. Tawney, *Religion and the Rise of Capitalism*, London, John Murray, 1926.
7. Reinhold Niebuhr, *Moral Man and Immoral Society*, New York, Scribner, 1932.